The Virtual Vanguards

Exploring the Evolution of Digital Diplomacy

Rahul Pawar & Ishwar Singh

ISBN 978-93-5667-890-3

Published in India 2023 by Pencil

Contributors:
Co-Author: Kanchan Pawar
Co-Author: Birinder Pal Kaur

A brand of
One Point Six Technologies Pvt. Ltd.
Unit no. 26, Ground Floor, Building A1,
Wadala Truck Terminal Road,
Near Post Office, Antop Hill, Mumbai - 400037
E connect@thepencilapp.com
W www.thepencilapp.com

Author biography

Throughout his career, Ishwar has published numerous influential papers and authored several books on political theory, comparative politics, and public policy. His research has shed light on issues such as democratic governance, political ideologies, social movements, and the impact of globalization on politics. His insightful analysis and ability to connect theoretical frameworks with real-world phenomena have earned him acclaim within the academic community.

Ishwar Singh's contributions to the field of political science have been widely recognized. He has received numerous accolades and awards for his outstanding research and teaching. His work has not only advanced the academic understanding of political science but has also influenced policymakers and practitioners in their decision-making processes.

After completing his formal education, Rahul embarked on a career as a computer scientist, dedicating himself to research and development. He joined a prominent technology company, where he worked on cutting-edge projects that pushed the boundaries of innovation. Rahul's expertise in machine learning and artificial intelligence allowed him to make significant breakthroughs in the development of intelligent systems and algorithms.

Rahul has published numerous research papers in esteemed journals, sharing his findings and advancements with the scientific community. His work has focused on leveraging machine learning techniques to solve complex problems, improve decision-making processes, and enhance the efficiency of systems.

CONTENTS

Epigraph

"A new frontier in diplomacy is opening up in the world of pixels and protocols. The art of statesmanship evolves as society embraces the digital era, becoming a digital dance of links and codes. The Virtual Vanguards appear, traversing the virtual world to influence dialogue throughout the world and create significant alliances. The power of diplomacy is in the hands of individuals who are fluent in the language of the virtual world in this era of digital diplomacy, when screens have taken the place of boardrooms and tweets are heard above speeches. Welcome to the age when digital influence reigns supreme and politicians design a new world order."

Foreword

The globe has experienced a stunning transition, both in terms of how we communicate and how we participate in international politics, in an era when technology and interconnection rule supreme. There is a new frontier that transcends geography and defies conventional concepts of diplomacy as our physical boundaries grow more permeable. Welcoming to the digital era of diplomacy.

The book "The Virtual Vanguards: Exploring the Evolution of Digital Diplomacy" examines the tremendous effects of technology on the profession of diplomacy in a relevant and thought-provoking manner. The pioneers who have embraced the digital sphere as a tool for international relations are highlighted in this ground-breaking study by the writers, who dive deeply into the complexities of this quickly changing terrain.

Once limited to opulent embassies and secret deliberations, diplomacy today reaches the farthest reaches of the world, seamlessly connecting people, communities, and countries. The whole nature of diplomacy is changing as social media platforms, virtual conferences, and online forums emerge as the new venues for communication. It's an exciting time for invention and adaptability, and the forerunners of the digital revolution are now leading the way.

"The Virtual Vanguards" takes us on a trip by illustrating the development of digital diplomacy from its infancy to the sophisticated stage it is in now. The writers shed light on the tactics used by digital diplomats, the difficulties they encounter, and the enormous chances they take advantage of via thorough study and perceptive analysis. They look at the development of digital ambassadors, the use of social media as a diplomatic instrument, and the ground-breaking projects that have reshaped the parameters of conventional diplomacy.

Understanding the strength and promise of technology is crucial as we negotiate the complicated world of digital diplomacy. It has the power to close gaps, magnify voices, and promote deep ties across cultures and countries. However, it also brings with it a whole set of problems and dangers, including the dissemination of false information, cyberattacks, and the diminution of privacy. The fair analysis of these complex topics in "The Virtual Vanguards" encourages readers to assess the ramifications of digital diplomacy.

For diplomats, academics, and decision-makers who want to comprehend the revolutionary effects of technology on international relations, this book is an invaluable resource. It challenges us to reexamine established norms, welcome innovation, and make the most of technological advances in order to create a society that is more diverse and interconnected. We learn priceless lessons on how to manage this constantly shifting environment and take advantage of the enormous potential it offers by studying the experiences and ideas of the virtual vanguards.

The book "The Virtual Vanguards: Exploring the Evolution of Digital Diplomacy" pushes us to rethink diplomacy in the digital era and welcomes us on a voyage of exploration. Through its pages, we learn about people who have pioneered new avenues for diplomatic engagement in the virtual world. We hope that this book will encourage everyone to embrace the potential of digital diplomacy and work toward a day when technology acts as a bridge that connects us all.

Birinder Pal Kaur

Preface

The field of diplomacy has seen a significant transition in an age marked by quick technical breakthroughs and linked global networks. Diplomacy itself has been redefined as the once solely physical domain of international interactions has entered the digital era. The aim of "The Virtual Vanguards: Exploring the Evolution of Digital Diplomacy" is to explore the unexplored waters of this developing topic within this framework.

As information continues to move freely across borders and through time and space, governments are presented with new possibilities and obstacles in their pursuit of successful diplomatic engagement. With the help of social media, internet platforms, and cutting-edge communication technology, digital diplomacy has grown to unparalleled heights of connectedness, communication, and impact.

"The Virtual Vanguards" explores the core of this changing environment and sheds insight on the main motivations, tactics, and effects of digital diplomacy. We want to document the variety of strategies used by countries, organizations, and people in their digital diplomatic activities by analyzing case studies from across the world. The book examines the many facets of this dynamic subject, ranging from the skillful use of social media campaigns to organize public opinion to the harnessing of big data analytics to impact policy choices.

It's crucial to understand the inherent complexity and moral questions that come with this digital transformation as we set out on our trip through the virtual halls of diplomacy. Although digital diplomacy has a lot of potential, it also presents significant obstacles including the spread of misinformation, the loss of privacy, and the digital gap that exacerbates already-existing inequities. "The Virtual Vanguards" urges politicians, diplomats, and people to critically evaluate the dangers and benefits of this new paradigm in order to provide a fair analysis of these concerns.

This book is not intended to be the last word on digital diplomacy since the field is always changing and so is our knowledge of it. The goal of "The Virtual Vanguards" is to start a debate that cuts beyond boundaries, fields of study, and viewpoints. By encouraging a diverse and international interchange of ideas, we seek to aid in the creation of ethical and practical digital diplomatic techniques that advance everyone's interests.

Finally, we would like to express our appreciation to the numerous diplomats, academics, and practitioners who kindly provided their perspectives and experiences, allowing us to shine light on this emerging topic. We encourage readers to approach this intellectual journey with an open mind, accepting the seemingly endless possibilities and confronting the difficult problems that digital diplomacy poses. Let's set out on a trip that will influence how international relations develop in the digital era together.

Rahul Pawar & Ishwar Singh

Acknowledgements

We would like to express our sincere gratitude and appreciation to our beloved parents, Smt. Amarjit Kaur, Shri Pal Singh, Smt. Saroj Pawar, and Shri Tilak Pawar, for their unfailing support, love, and encouragement during our journey to research and write this book. Our success has been greatly aided by their advice and support, and we will always be grateful to them for their tremendous efforts.

First and foremost, we want to express our gratitude to Smt. Amarjit Kaur and Smt. Saroj Pawar, our moms. Our lives have been supported by their love and sacrifice. They have consistently served as our pillars of support, inspiration, and comprehension. Our ability to overcome obstacles and achieve our academic goals has been fueled by their unwavering support and faith in our skills.

We owe a debt of appreciation to our dads, Shri Pal Singh and Shri Tilak Pawar, for their priceless advice and knowledge. They have continuously served as an inspiration to us, showing us the value of tenacity, diligence, and commitment. Our paths and aspirations have been significantly shaped and nurtured by their constant support and faith in our goals.

We also want to express our gratitude to our parents for giving up things in order to provide us the greatest educational opportunity. To make sure we had access to high-quality education and resources, they worked diligently and even made personal sacrifices. Our strong feeling of appreciation and desire to live up to their standards have been inspired by their selflessness and devotion.

We are appreciative of our parents for creating a culture that values education and curiosity. They fostered our intellectual development from an early age, motivating us to look into new concepts, challenge the existing quo, and become passionate about learning. Their unshakable faith in the value of education has helped to mold us into critical thinkers and lifelong learners.

Additionally, we would want to express our sincere gratitude for the many sacrifices our parents have made in order to provide for us materially, morally, and emotionally. They have always been our pillars of support, providing direction in trying times and exulting in our victories as no one else can. Their unshakable faith in our competence has given us the courage to follow our aspirations bravely.

We also want to thank our parents for their incredible tolerance and understanding during this process. They have given advice, been a listening ear, and given the emotional support required to go through the highs and lows of academic research. Even in our self-doubt, their confidence in us has been a tremendous source of support.

We also like to thank our parents for their support and interest in our academic endeavors. Our research interests have been significantly shaped by their constant encouragement to investigate new areas, participate in thought-provoking debates, and pursue greatness. Our enthusiasm for examining how computer science affects political campaigns has been stoked by their faith in the ability of education to bring about good change.

For their incalculable contributions to our life and this thesis, our parents, Smt. Amarjit Kaur, Shri Pal Singh, Smt. Saroj Pawar, and Shri Tilak Pawar, deserve the deepest gratitude. This scientific project would not have been feasible without their unfailing support, love, and advice. They have been a continual source of inspiration and strength in our lives. We dedicate this thesis to our parents in appreciation of the tireless work they did to mold us into the people we are today. May we always strive to honor them in whatever we do.

The Virtual Vanguards

Chapter 1

Introduction

The arrival of the digital era has caused a significant upheaval in the field of diplomacy. The internet's broad usage and the quick growth of technology have completely changed how countries connect and handle diplomatic relations. A new kind of diplomacy known as "digital diplomacy" has emerged as a result of this transformation, and it makes use of the power of digital tools and platforms to improve international interaction, cooperation, and communication.

The comprehensive research "The Virtual Vanguards: Exploring the Evolution of Digital Diplomacy" aims to evaluate and comprehend the numerous facets of digital diplomacy, its origin, and its influence on conventional diplomatic procedures. This thorough investigation will shed light on the pivotal role that technology will play in determining the direction of diplomacy in the future, as well as the possibilities and difficulties it brings.

Digital technologies, including social media, online platforms, data analytics, and artificial intelligence, are used in "digital diplomacy" to accomplish diplomatic goals and develop world relations. It includes a broad variety of activities, such as digital advocacy, virtual summits, e-diplomacy, and cyber diplomacy. A number of variables, including as the broad availability of internet connection, the rising usage of social media, and the need for more effective and inclusive diplomatic methods, may be used to explain the fast expansion of digital diplomacy.

The rising significance of public diplomacy in the digital era is one of the main forces behind digital diplomacy. Public diplomacy has traditionally meant interacting with international audiences to advance a nation's policies, beliefs, and culture. Governments and diplomats may now interact directly with global audiences, avoiding conventional media gatekeepers, thanks to the growth of social media platforms. As a result, diplomacy has become more democratic, providing a wider variety of players—including people, non-state actors, and civil society organizations—a voice. Digital platforms are becoming effective instruments for rallying support, influencing public opinion, and affecting policy decisions.

The use of virtual platforms for diplomatic encounters is an important part of digital diplomacy. Today's leaders and diplomats may interact and work together across borders without having to physically travel thanks to virtual summits and online conferences. Due to the reduction of geographical boundaries and logistical challenges, these virtual meetings have enhanced the frequency and accessibility of diplomatic interactions while also enabling more inclusive participation. Additionally, by offering a forum for discussion, negotiation, and coordination, virtual platforms have encouraged multilateral collaboration on global issues including climate change, cybersecurity, and public health.

Using data analytics and artificial intelligence, digital diplomacy has also changed conventional diplomatic procedures. Big data and sophisticated analytics are being used more often by governments and diplomats to understand public mood, spot patterns, and adjust their message and strategy as necessary. Large volumes of data can be processed by machine learning algorithms, allowing diplomats to study social media discussions, spot misinformation efforts, and foresee new trends. Additionally, chatbots and virtual assistants powered by artificial intelligence are being used to give information, respond to inquiries, and improve diplomatic services.

While digital diplomacy has a wealth of benefits, it also comes with dangers and problems that need to be managed. As governments and diplomats communicate sensitive information online and connect with one other digitally, cybersecurity and data privacy issues are of utmost importance. To protect sensitive data and diplomatic communications against cyberattacks, hacking, and data breaches, strict security standards and safeguards are required. Furthermore, the digital gap still poses a serious problem since not all countries and communities have access to digital technology and internet connection on an equal basis. This disparity may worsen existing power disparities and restrict the inclusiveness and efficacy of digital diplomacy initiatives.

To explore these facets of digital diplomacy and consider its effects on international relations, the book "The Virtual Vanguards: Exploring the Evolution of Digital Diplomacy" was written. This research will provide important insights into the changing nature of diplomacy and the role that technology will play in determining its future by examining case studies, best practices, and policy frameworks from across the globe. It will also examine the moral and legal implications of digital diplomacy, such as concerns about responsibility, privacy, and the possibility of algorithmic prejudice.

In conclusion, digital diplomacy has become a significant influence on the development of modern diplomatic procedures. The increased use of digital technology has created new opportunities for international participation, cooperation, and communication. The goal of "The Virtual Vanguards: Exploring the Evolution of Digital Diplomacy" is to examine the many elements of digital diplomacy and highlight its potential for transformation. This research will help us comprehend how diplomacy is changing in the digital era by evaluating its prospects, difficulties, and repercussions.

Chapter 2

Diplomacy in the Digital Age

2. Introduction

The digital era has altered many parts of our lives in today's linked world, including diplomacy. Technology breakthroughs and the emergence of the digital age have had a significant impact on diplomacy, which is conventionally described as the art and practice of conducting discussions between representatives of governments. The digital era has changed the nature of international relations and how diplomats conduct themselves, in addition to expanding the avenues through which diplomatic communication occurs. This paradigm change has created both possibilities and problems, forcing diplomats to adapt and adopt new tools and methods in order to successfully negotiate the challenging terrain of diplomacy in the digital era.

The revolution of communication is one of the biggest transformations the digital age has brought about. The emergence of the internet, social networking sites, and instant messaging services has increased global connectivity like never before. With the capacity to communicate with peers across the globe in real time, geographical and time zone constraints are no longer an issue for diplomats. This instantaneous communication has quickened the speed of diplomacy, enabling prompt replies and cutting down on the amount of time needed to secure accords. A more participatory and open diplomatic procedure is now possible because to the direct involvement between diplomats and civilians made possible by digital communication tools.

The internet era has also made it possible for individuals and non-state entities to engage in diplomatic dialogue. Social media sites like Twitter and Facebook have developed into effective public diplomacy tools that provide diplomats the ability to interact directly with a worldwide audience and influence public opinion. This change has increased the reach of diplomacy while simultaneously democratizing it, giving disadvantaged populations a voice and promoting more openness and accountability in international interactions.

However, the digital era has also presented diplomats with new difficulties and complexity. It has become more and more challenging to sort through the clutter and find trustworthy sources as a result of the large quantity of information that is now accessible online. In order to successfully assess and understand digital information, diplomats must learn to discern between reliable sources and propaganda or misinformation. Furthermore, cyber dangers, such as information warfare and hacking efforts, have turned the digital world into a battlefield. To safeguard sensitive information and maintain the integrity of diplomatic communication, diplomats must be well-versed in cybersecurity concepts and techniques.

The development of digital diplomacy, often known as e-diplomacy, is an important part of diplomacy in the digital era. The use of digital tools and technology to advance diplomatic endeavors and accomplish foreign policy objectives is referred to as "digital diplomacy." It entails actions like online negotiations, virtual conferences, and digital public diplomacy initiatives. E-diplomacy gives ambassadors new ways to interact with stakeholders, promote global collaboration, and solve pressing issues. It also makes room for cutting-edge methods of diplomacy, such track-two diplomacy, which incorporates think tanks and non-governmental entities in diplomatic efforts. Diplomats now have access to a wider variety of instruments in the digital era, which may be used in addition to more conventional diplomatic techniques.

Additionally, new diplomatic players have emerged in the digital era. The development of international relations is now heavily influenced by technology firms, multinational enterprises, and non-governmental organizations (NGOs). These players may have an effect on diplomatic procedures and results because they have enormous resources, knowledge, and power. Now, diplomats must interact with these players, build alliances with them, and take use of their potential to advance national interests and tackle global issues. The public-private divide has become more hazy in the digital era, demanding a collaborative and multi-stakeholder approach to diplomacy.

Along with these adjustments, the digital era has brought up significant concerns about sovereignty, data protection, and privacy. The security and confidentiality of sensitive information are issues as a result of the growing dependence on digital channels for diplomatic communication. Diplomats must manage the ethical and legal ramifications of data protection to maintain the confidentiality and security of diplomatic communication. Additionally, since digital activities cross international boundaries and are governed by several legal systems, the digital age has put conventional ideas of sovereignty to the test. In order to preserve the interests and rights of nations in the digital sphere, diplomats must confront these complicated concerns and advocate for international norms and rules.

Diplomacy is changing drastically in the digital era. The digital revolution has opened up new diplomatic communication channels, given people and non-state actors more influence, and given diplomats new tools and approaches. The need to navigate new diplomatic players and concerns, cybersecurity risks, and information overload are just a few of the difficulties it has brought about. Diplomats need to develop their digital literacy, cybersecurity knowledge, and interpersonal skills in order to adapt to this fast changing environment. The digital era has enormous opportunities for strengthening diplomacy and tackling global issues, but it also necessitates that diplomats find a careful balance between using technology and respecting the values and conventions that guide international relations. Diplomacy can only prosper in the digital era by seizing the possibilities and conquering the difficulties.

2.1 Understanding the digital revolution and its impact on diplomacy

Communication, business, and government are just a few of the areas of human existence that have been altered by the digital revolution. The emergence of digital technology has significantly altered how countries engage with one another and carry out their foreign policy in the field of diplomacy. The goal of this article is to examine the digital revolution and its enormous effects on diplomacy, stressing the main changes that have occurred in diplomatic procedures, the difficulties that diplomats now confront, and any possibilities that could result from using digital tools in diplomacy.

The fast development of digital technology, especially the internet, which has transformed how individuals access and exchange information, is referred to as the "digital revolution." By shifting communication channels, improving information exchange, and changing the dynamics of power and influence in international relations, this revolution has had a significant effect on diplomacy. With the widespread use of the internet and the rise of social media platforms, diplomacy has expanded into the digital sphere and is no longer limited to conventional routes, allowing for direct connection between diplomats and individuals on both sides of international boundaries.

By allowing diplomats to participate in public diplomacy, which entails directly engaging foreign publics, the digital revolution has changed conventional diplomatic procedures. Social media sites like Twitter and Facebook have developed into effective tools for diplomats to spread government messages, interact with audiences abroad, and influence public opinion. Bypassing conventional gatekeepers and middlemen, this direct interaction promotes more transparency and openness in international relations.

Digital technology have also encouraged e-diplomacy, in which diplomats use electronic tools for information collection, negotiation, and communication. As common forms of diplomatic interaction, video conferences, online forums, and virtual summits have emerged, they have given diplomats additional chances to communicate with their colleagues and conduct talks afar. Digital platforms have also made it easier to share information, research, and diplomatic papers, improving the efficacy and efficiency of diplomatic procedures.

While the digital revolution has greatly aided diplomacy, it has also created new difficulties. The problem of cybersecurity is one such difficulty. The susceptibility to cyber assaults becomes a key worry as diplomacy depends more and more on digital platforms and information systems. State-sponsored hackers or non-state actors looking to acquire classified material or obstruct diplomatic procedures may attack diplomatic posts and sensitive communications. Therefore, to preserve sensitive information and defend their digital infrastructure, diplomats must implement strong cybersecurity procedures.

The spread of false information and fake news in the digital age is another problem. Due to the ease with which information can be shared on social media, malevolent actors are able to mislead the public and sway opinion, weakening diplomatic efforts. The need for critical thinking and digital literacy in diplomacy is furthered by the fact that diplomats must wade through a sea of false information and devise plans to combat disinformation efforts.

The digital revolution offers huge prospects for diplomacy notwithstanding its difficulties. Diplomats may interact with a variety of stakeholders, including youth, marginalized populations, and civil society organizations, thanks to the increased inclusion and broader reach of digital platforms. By embracing many viewpoints and promoting inclusion, this increased engagement improves diplomatic decision-making processes.

Additionally, data analytics and artificial intelligence (AI) provide diplomats with new tools to evaluate massive volumes of data, spot trends, and come to more educated conclusions. AI-powered algorithms may support social media sentiment monitoring, trend forecasting, and emergent problem detection, allowing diplomats to react proactively and successfully influence public opinion. The capacity to gather, evaluate, and use data for fact-based policymaking and diplomatic discussions is also improved by digital technology.

Without a question, the digital revolution has changed diplomacy, changing established procedures and altering the dynamics of international interactions. Now that diplomats have unparalleled access to international audiences, they may engage in direct dialogue and take part in public diplomacy projects. The growth of false information and cybersecurity concerns are two issues that this digital shift also raises. Diplomats may overcome these difficulties and use digital technologies to strengthen their diplomatic efforts by embracing the possibilities given by the digital age, such as inclusion and data-driven decision-making. Diplomats must adapt as the digital revolution progresses and take use of its potential to successfully promote their nations' interests in a fast changing international environment.

2.2 The emergence of digital diplomacy as a distinct field

The phrase "digital diplomacy," which was first used in the early 21st century, describes how diplomatic players utilize digital platforms and technology to conduct diplomatic operations, improve international relations, and promote national interests. Diplomacy changed to fit this new environment as the globe grew more linked and dependent on digital instruments. The rise of digital diplomacy as a unique discipline, its effects on conventional diplomatic procedures, and the potential and problems it brings are all discussed in this article.

There are a number of reasons why digital diplomacy has become so popular. First and foremost, technological developments have altered how individuals connect and communicate. The growth of the internet, social media sites, and mobile technology has opened up new channels for diplomatic interaction. Governments were aware of the potential of digital technologies in the early 2000s to reach a wider audience, distribute information, and influence public opinion. They therefore started including internet channels in their diplomatic approaches.

Public diplomacy, e-diplomacy, cyber diplomacy, and virtual diplomacy are only a few of the many activities that fall under the umbrella of "digital diplomacy." Using digital platforms to interact with international audiences, advance national interests, and forge connections is known as public diplomacy. Governments use websites, blogs, and social media platforms to exchange information, create narratives, and have conversations. E-diplomacy is the practice of conducting diplomatic discussions by email, video conferencing, and other online communication methods. Concerns about cybersecurity, cyberthreats, and international digital collaboration are the main topics of cyber diplomacy. Conducting summits, conferences, and discussions on a virtual level is known as virtual diplomacy.

Traditional diplomatic methods have significantly changed as a result of the emergence of digital diplomacy. Diplomacy has become more democratic, which is a major improvement. Non-state actors, such as civil society groups, activists, and individuals, now have more authority to hold diplomatic conversations thanks to digital platforms. Diplomacy used to be solely the purview of diplomats and government representatives, but nowadays, civilians may influence foreign policy discussions and advance their own interests. Additionally, digital diplomacy has sped up information exchange and communication, allowing diplomats to react quickly to developing problems and crises.

There are several potential for diplomatic players in digital diplomacy. It enables governments to communicate with foreign publics directly while avoiding conventional media gatekeepers and reaching a global audience. This improved public diplomacy may promote understanding among people, cross cultural barriers, and develop trust. Additionally, digital platforms allow for virtual communication and cooperation between nations, enabling diplomatic endeavors to transcend geographical barriers. Additionally, with the use of digital technologies, diplomatic techniques may be improved by facilitating data-driven decision-making, policy research, and public mood monitoring.

However, there are difficulties with digital diplomacy. The possibility for false information and the propagation of disinformation operations is a major worry. The complicated terrain of false news, internet trolls, and information warfare must be negotiated by governments. It is a difficult effort to keep diplomatic communication credible in a time of information overload and internet echo chambers. Digital diplomacy also brings up issues with security and privacy. Using digital channels exclusively for diplomatic communication leaves private data open to cyber attacks and spying.

Looking forward, it is expected that digital diplomacy will keep developing and affecting diplomatic procedures. Emerging industries like blockchain and artificial intelligence (AI) might significantly affect diplomatic operations as technology develops. Data analysis, policy creation, and preemptive diplomacy may all be aided by AI. Blockchain technology has the ability to improve diplomatic transactions' security, trustworthiness, and transparency. Additionally, by providing immersive and participatory experiences, the combination of virtual reality and augmented reality may improve diplomatic discussions and cultural exchanges.

The practice of diplomacy in the twenty-first century has changed as a result of the development of digital diplomacy as a separate subject. Diplomatic actors must adjust to this quickly changing environment as digital tools and platforms continue to develop. While digital diplomacy brings exciting possibilities for international participation, it also has problems with security, privacy, and information integrity. In the years to come, digital diplomacy may play a crucial role in influencing international relations and fostering mutual understanding by using the potential of digital technology while tackling these difficulties.

2.3 Exploring the opportunities and challenges presented by digital technologies in diplomacy

Diplomacy is no exception to how digital technology have transformed other facets of human existence. Digital technology' quick development and broad usage have created both possibilities and difficulties for diplomatic efforts. This article will examine the advantages and disadvantages of using digital technologies in diplomacy and how they affect global relations. We will examine how advancements in digital technology have altered conventional diplomatic procedures, improved communication channels, expedited the exchange of information, and impacted decision-making procedures. We'll also talk about the difficulties of digital diplomacy, including cybersecurity risks, information overload, and the digital divide.

Digital technologies provide many prospects for diplomacy and give diplomats the chance to use more effective and efficient methods. First, the development of digital diplomacy has improved lines of communication, enabling diplomats to interact instantly with peers across boundaries. Diplomats have access to real-time communication capabilities via platforms like video conferencing, email, and social media, enabling rapid answers and minimizing the need for actual travel.

Digital technology have also increased the effect and reach of diplomatic efforts. Diplomats may interact directly with a worldwide audience through social media platforms, altering perceptions and influencing public opinion. This public diplomacy strategy enables ambassadors to cross cultural divides, forge connections, and spread information more widely. Additionally, digital platforms provide chances for virtual diplomacy, in which diplomats may have conversations and debates via the internet while saving money and expanding accessibility.

Digital technology have also made it easier for diplomats to share information and make better diplomatic decisions. Diplomats may quickly acquire pertinent information thanks to the accessibility of enormous volumes of data, real-time information, and analytical tools, assisting in the formulation of well-informed decisions. Digital platforms have also made it simpler for diplomats and the general public to access and study diplomatic agreements, declarations, and other official papers, increasing the openness of diplomatic actions.

Digital technologies provide enormous potential for diplomacy, but they also present important problems that must be solved. The problem of cybersecurity is one of the main difficulties. Cyberattacks, espionage, and data breaches may affect diplomatic communication and data. Strong cybersecurity procedures, standards, and international collaboration are required to protect diplomatic networks and information systems from these attacks.

Additionally, diplomats may experience information overload as a result of the quantity of digital material, which makes it difficult for them to sift and prioritize pertinent information. Diplomats must acquire the abilities necessary to go through the enormous quantity of material accessible and draw insightful conclusions. Additionally, diplomatic efforts are hampered by the transmission of false and misleading information on digital channels. Diplomats must devise plans to combat false narratives and guarantee the veracity and authenticity of the information supplied.

Digital technology may also widen the gap in diplomacy between those who have access to knowledge and resources and those who don't. The ability of developing nations or areas to fully participate in digital diplomacy initiatives may be hindered by their limited access to digital infrastructure and technology resources. International collaboration, investments in digital infrastructure, and capacity development are necessary to close the digital gap.

With the advent of digital technology, diplomatic procedures may now be made more effective and efficient. The way ambassadors conduct business has been completely transformed by our capacity to communicate instantly, interact with a worldwide audience, and access massive quantities of information. However, there are difficulties with digital diplomacy as well, such as cybersecurity risks, information overload, and the digital divide. International collaboration, strong cybersecurity safeguards, enhanced information management techniques, and initiatives to close the digital gap are all necessary for addressing these difficulties.

Diplomacy must adjust as digital technologies develop in order to take use of their possibilities and address their problems. Diplomats may better negotiate the challenges of the digital age, advance international collaboration, and promote understanding in a world that is becoming more linked by adopting digital diplomacy.

Chapter 3

The Rise of Virtual Embassies

3. Introduction

The idea of conventional embassies is changing in the current day, as technology permeates every part of our life. International relations are being transformed by the emergence of virtual embassies, which are reinventing diplomatic procedures. In an increasingly linked world, virtual embassies promote communication and collaboration by bridging the gap between states and conducting diplomatic operations. This article examines how virtual embassies have developed, their benefits and drawbacks, and any future repercussions for international relations and global government.

Definition and Development of Virtual Embassies: The construction of diplomatic missions online that use digital platforms and technologies rather than physical infrastructure is referred to as a virtual embassy. The goal of virtual embassies is to provide a digital forum for diplomatic exchanges, promoting dialogue and international cooperation. They provide an alternative to conventional embassies with physical locations while removing geographic restrictions and lowering operations expenses.

Early attempts concentrated on creating embassy websites to convey information and interact with the public, but the concept of virtual embassies has developed through time. Virtual embassies, however, have evolved into full platforms for diplomacy, commerce, cultural exchange, and consular services as a result of technical breakthroughs like the introduction of social media, video conferencing, and virtual reality.

Benefits of Virtual Embassies: Traditional embassies often find it difficult to give the same benefits that virtual embassies do. They first offer 24-hour accessibility, enabling people to communicate with diplomats and use consular services without being constrained by time zones or geography. Accessibility improves diplomatic relations and speeds up crisis response and support to foreign nationals.

Second, virtual embassies have financial advantages. Virtual embassies are able to spend resources more effectively and concentrate on their primary diplomatic functions since they don't need physical facilities and incur less operating costs. Governments may build a presence and reach a wider audience using this strategy in places where establishing actual embassies could be difficult or expensive.

Thirdly, electronic embassies promote diversity and democratic diplomacy. They provide a venue for communication with a broader variety of stakeholders, including as non-governmental organizations (NGOs), civil society groups, and those who may not have easy access to conventional diplomatic channels. By encouraging openness, engagement, and public diplomacy, virtual embassies may strengthen the credibility and efficiency of diplomatic activities.

Virtual embassies carry out a variety of diplomatic tasks in a manner that is comparable to those of their physical counterparts. They enhance the protection of people overseas by fostering bilateral and international cooperation and facilitating communication and negotiation between governments. Virtual embassies may also serve as centers of economic diplomacy, promoting commercial ties and luring foreign direct investment.

Additionally, virtual embassies thrive in public diplomacy initiatives, utilizing websites, social media platforms, and virtual events to interact with the public, provide cultural knowledge, and advance international understanding. They may hold online conferences, cultural fairs, and educational events, enhancing intercultural dialogue and promoting cooperation on a worldwide scale.

Challenges & Limitations: Despite the many benefits, virtual embassies are subject to several difficulties and restrictions. Among the main issues is cybersecurity. Strong cybersecurity measures are essential to prevent cyberattacks and safeguard diplomatic communications since virtual embassies depend on digital infrastructure and handle sensitive information.

The possibility for digital exclusion is another difficulty. Despite the widespread use of the internet, not all areas and groups have widespread access to modern technology. The usefulness of virtual embassies in reaching out to communities without connection or technology knowledge may be hampered by this digital gap.

Furthermore, it might be difficult for virtual embassies to build credibility and confidence. In order to create credibility and foster connections, traditional diplomatic techniques have historically focused on physical presence and face-to-face meetings. Virtual embassies must negotiate these forces and devise plans to win over the confidence and respect of authorities, international organizations, and the general public.

The emergence of virtual embassies has significant ramifications for international relations and global government. The conventional diplomatic paradigm may be changed by virtual embassies to make it more flexible, inclusive, and responsive to the digital era. They may speed up decision-making by facilitating direct contact between governments, cutting through established bureaucratic routes.

Additionally, by giving countries a platform for greater interaction, virtual embassies may promote international collaboration and diplomacy. They may encourage communication, help resolve disputes, and spread information about pressing issues like public health, cybersecurity, and climate change.

Multilateral organizations have the opportunity to expand their diplomatic reach via the use of virtual embassies.

Organizations like the United Nations may use virtual platforms to interact more directly and actively with stakeholders like member states and civil society. This strategy may improve global governance and fulfill the changing demands and expectations of a globally networked society.

With the use of digital tools and platforms to get over physical and operational constraints, the advent of virtual embassies represents a fundamental change in how diplomacy is practiced. The accessibility, cost-effectiveness, and inclusiveness of virtual embassies are only a few of their many benefits, but they also have problems with cybersecurity, digital exclusion, and trust-building. However, their development has the potential to revolutionize global government and diplomacy by promoting open dialogue, encouraging collaboration, and allowing more flexible and inclusive diplomatic procedures in the digital era.

3.1 Examining the concept of virtual embassies and their significance

Technology breakthroughs are transforming conventional diplomacy in today's more linked world. The idea of virtual embassies, which makes use of digital platforms to promote diplomatic interaction and communication, is one noteworthy innovation. Virtual embassies are online counterparts to real-world embassies that allow diplomats to carry out diplomatic operations. The purpose of this article is to investigate the idea of virtual embassies, analyze its relevance, and speculate on how it could affect future diplomatic relations.

In response to the increasing dependence on the internet and electronic communication technologies, the idea of virtual embassies was developed. The necessity to modify diplomatic procedures became obvious with the quick rise of internet access and the extensive use of social media. By bridging the physical gap between countries, virtual embassies enable ambassadors to communicate in real time with foreign governments, people, and enterprises from anywhere in the world.

Virtual embassies provide a variety of features and functions that mimic the offerings of conventional physical embassies. These include of crisis management, public diplomacy, commerce promotion, cultural exchange initiatives, and consular services. Diplomats may help with visa applications, provide consular support, and promote contact between individuals and their home governments using online platforms. In order to improve international relations, virtual embassies may also foster bilateral commerce, present a country's culture, and take part in public diplomacy activities.

The importance of virtual embassies is as follows:

a. Enhanced Diplomatic Access: Through virtual embassies, one may increase diplomatic engagement and access. Diplomats may reach a larger audience by using digital technology, including rural areas and disenfranchised people that would have difficult physical access to conventional embassies. The values of democracy and diplomacy are promoted by this improved accessibility, which also promotes inclusion and guarantees that all people have access to diplomatic services.

b. Cost-Effectiveness and Efficiency: Maintaining physical embassies may be expensive for nations, particularly those with few financial resources. By lowering the infrastructure expenditures, personnel needs, and operating costs related to maintaining a physical presence in several places, virtual embassies provide a cost-effective option. Additionally, the use of digital platforms enables ambassadors to carry out several diplomatic tasks at once, improving efficiency and resource allocation.

c. Real-Time Diplomatic Engagement: Conventional diplomatic processes can include drawn-out bureaucratic channels and time-consuming procedures. These procedures are streamlined by virtual embassies, which make real-time contact and quick information exchange possible. This promotes quicker and more successful diplomacy by hastening decision-making, facilitating crisis management, and enhancing diplomatic discussions.

d. worldwide Reach and Influence: Virtual embassies may increase a country's influence and worldwide reach. Diplomats may interact with international audiences online, build relationships, and influence public opinion outside of their own country's boundaries. A country's ability to represent its values, culture, and policies on a worldwide level is strengthened by this increased reach. Virtual embassies may use the potential of digital diplomacy to advance national interests and have an impact on world events by using social media.

Virtual embassies have many benefits, but they also have problems and restrictions that need to be worked around:

a. technology Barriers: Reliable internet infrastructure and cutting-edge technology skills are needed for the effective operation of virtual embassies. Many nations, especially those in developing areas, do not have sufficient connectivity or technical resources. For excluded groups to have fair access to virtual diplomatic services and to avoid exclusion, this digital gap must be closed.

b. Privacy and Cybersecurity Issues: Data breaches and cybersecurity concerns may affect virtual embassies. To safeguard national interests and sensitive information, diplomatic communication and information must be secure. To reduce the hazards related to virtual diplomacy, robust cybersecurity standards and encryption technologies are required. To preserve confidence and secure personal information, it is also necessary to address privacy and data protection issues.

c. Absence of Face-to-Face Communication: While virtual embassies provide convenience and efficiency, they lack the direct communication that comes with face-to-face communication. Virtual diplomacy may lose the nonverbal indications, cultural quirks, and diplomatic procedure that are essential to actual diplomacy. To maintain the human aspect in diplomatic contacts, it is crucial to maintain a balance between virtual and physical diplomacy.

Future diplomatic efforts might greatly benefit from the idea of virtual embassies:

a. Geopolitical Dynamics: By enabling nations to strengthen diplomatic connections and have communication regardless of geographical distance, virtual embassies may influence geopolitical dynamics. This may encourage regional collaboration, help resolve conflicts, and result in the establishment of new alliances.

b. Innovation and Adaptability in Diplomacy: The advent of virtual embassies illustrates the necessity for innovation and acclimatization in diplomacy. Diplomats must adapt to these changes as technology develops and take use of the possibilities offered by online platforms. A forum for testing out novel diplomatic strategies, such as digital diplomacy, citizen engagement, and public involvement, is offered by virtual embassies.

c. Inclusion and Participation: Through virtual embassies, citizens may participate more actively in diplomatic operations. Citizens may participate in public diplomacy activities, provide comments on policies, and participate in decision-making by using digital technologies. This interactive method encourages inclusion, accountability, and openness in diplomatic matters.

d. Diplomacy in Emergency Situations: Virtual embassies have proven useful in emergency situations, such as pandemics or natural catastrophes. Virtual embassies can successfully maintain diplomatic operations, provide consular services, and coordinate international responses when physical travel and communication are constrained.

A substantial change in diplomatic procedures, the idea of virtual embassies has several benefits, including improved accessibility, cost efficiency, and real-time involvement. However, it is crucial to address the issues with technology, cybersecurity, and the maintenance of interpersonal communication. Virtual embassies have the ability to transform diplomacy, encourage international cooperation, and advance inclusion and creativity in diplomatic matters as technology develops. Accepting the idea of virtual embassies might provide new diplomatic opportunities and enable meaningful interaction in a world that is becoming more linked.

3.2 Case studies of countries leveraging virtual embassies for diplomatic outreach

The idea of conventional embassies is changing quickly in the modern digital age because of technology breakthroughs and shifting communication patterns. A unique and creative method for conducting diplomatic outreach and advancing international relations has emerged: virtual embassies. Countries may create virtual embassies that cross geographical borders by using digital platforms and technology, allowing them to interact with global audiences in novel and engaging ways. This article examines case studies of nations that have effectively improved their diplomatic efforts by using virtual embassies, emphasizing their techniques, difficulties, and results.

Estonia, which is renowned for its technological innovations, has been a pioneer in using virtual embassies to increase its diplomatic influence. Estonia's virtual embassy network is built on the e-residence initiative, which provides digital residence to entrepreneurs and enterprises throughout the globe. Estonia actively advertises its e-Residency program via virtual embassies, luring foreign capital and developing partnerships with businesses throughout the world. The virtual embassies provide as a focal point for online interaction, providing potential e-residents with knowledge, assistance, and networking possibilities.

South Korea saw the potential of virtual embassies as a way to strengthen its cultural diplomacy and soft power initiatives. To promote Korean culture, language, and arts, the Korean Cultural Centers (KCCs) set up virtual embassies in a number of nations. Through digital channels, these virtual embassies interact with the local communities by holding online exhibits, concerts, and seminars. By using virtual embassies, South Korea efficiently promotes its cultural legacy, enhances intercultural communication, and promotes a favorable image of the nation abroad.

With virtual embassies as a potent instrument to increase trade and investment prospects, the Netherlands has benefited. The Dutch government built a network of virtual embassies that put an emphasis on economic diplomacy after realizing the shortcomings of conventional embassies. To promote commercial partnerships, these virtual embassies provide specialized information on trade policies, investment prospects, and market data. The virtual embassies of the Netherlands have been effective in luring foreign direct investment and promoting Dutch companies on a worldwide scale.

Australia has used virtual embassies as a powerful tool for enhancing public diplomacy initiatives and interacting with audiences throughout the world. Information on Australia's culture, education, tourism, and innovation may be shared via the nation's virtual embassies. Australia successfully communicates its beliefs, policies, and projects via interactive websites, social media platforms, and virtual events, encouraging people-to-people interactions and advancing a positive perception of the nation internationally.

In managing crises and assisting its residents overseas, the United Arab Emirates (UAE) has shown the strategic utility of virtual embassies. The virtual embassies of the UAE provide immediate support and information to people living or traveling abroad. Virtual embassies are essential for communication and cooperation during crises like natural catastrophes or political turmoil. The UAE has had success in reaching out to its residents and ensuring their safety and well-being by utilizing virtual embassies.

The US has deliberately used virtual embassies to broaden its attempts at international involvement after realizing the value of digital diplomacy. Through virtual embassies, online events, and the provision of digital materials on numerous issues, the U.S. Department of State has launched a digital outreach strategy. By adopting virtual embassies, the United States hopes to achieve its foreign policy objectives, foster intercultural understanding, and reach audiences in places where it has little physical presence.

Although virtual embassies have many benefits, setting one up has its difficulties and concerns. These include assuring data security and protection, dealing with possible impediments to online access, getting over linguistic and cultural difficulties, and juggling online interaction with actual diplomatic activities. Additionally, nations must manage the legal and regulatory concerns of virtual embassies and set up enough funding for their construction and upkeep.

The case studies in this article show how many nations have used virtual embassies in various ways for diplomatic outreach. In an increasingly linked world, virtual embassies have become an efficient way to expand diplomatic reach and interact with international audiences for a variety of purposes, from entrepreneurship promotion to cultural diplomacy, trade facilitation to crisis management. Virtual embassies will probably play a more and bigger part in determining the future of diplomacy, enabling worldwide cooperation, and promoting global understanding as technology develops.

3.3 Assessing the role of virtual embassies in shaping digital diplomacy

In the contemporary world, digital diplomacy has become a potent weapon that is reshaping established diplomatic procedures and creating new opportunities for interaction. The idea of virtual embassies, which enables nations to have an online presence that transcends geographical limits, is a noteworthy component of digital diplomacy.

Digital platforms and technology are used by virtual embassies to improve diplomatic ties by facilitating communication and encouraging cross-cultural engagement. This article examines the benefits, drawbacks, and probable repercussions for international relations of virtual embassies in defining digital diplomacy. This examination will provide a full knowledge of the effect and potential of virtual embassies by looking at case studies and academic research.

The manner that countries handle diplomatic relations has changed dramatically because to virtual embassies. Traditional embassies are physical establishments that promote their home nation's interests while promoting communication between governments. They are situated on foreign land. In contrast, virtual embassies only exist online and use the internet and cutting-edge technology to perform diplomatic duties. These internet platforms provide as entry points for digital diplomacy, allowing governments to communicate with audiences throughout the world, spread knowledge, and strengthen bilateral ties.

The landscape of digital diplomacy is shaped by the benefits that virtual embassies provide. First off, they provide a more affordable option to traditional embassies by lowering the costs of staffing, travel, and maintaining infrastructure. This makes it possible for nations, especially those with minimal resources, to establish diplomatic ties and participate in international affairs without having to bear heavy financial costs. Second, virtual embassies may reach audiences in far-off places or nations where they do not have physical representation by overcoming geographic boundaries. Greater inclusion is made possible by this worldwide accessibility, which also broadens the range of diplomatic interaction.

Diplomatic communication has changed dramatically as a result of digital diplomacy made possible by virtual embassies. Governments may deal directly and transparently with foreign communities thanks to these internet channels. Diplomats have the chance to offer cultural information, explain policy viewpoints, and answer to public inquiries via social media platforms, government websites, and virtual events. Such open lines of communication may strengthen public diplomacy initiatives by enabling governments to craft their story and create understanding with global audiences.

Virtual embassies are essential for fostering international cultural interaction. Countries may share with a worldwide audience their cultural traditions, creative expressions, and history via internet platforms. People from all backgrounds may discover and enjoy many cultures thanks to virtual exhibits, live performances, and digital archives. This cultural diplomacy, which is made possible by online embassies, promotes understanding, tolerance, and intercultural communication.

With the help of virtual embassies, international relations may be improved. Nations may communicate, bargain, and work together on a variety of problems by creating a virtual presence, regardless of physical separation. Diplomats may engage bilateral conversations, exchange ideas, and tackle common difficulties via virtual diplomatic meetings, video conferences, and online discussion forums. Virtual embassies may also promote relationships between individuals, allowing people to communicate with ambassadors and bridging the gap between countries.

Virtual embassies have many advantages, but they can have drawbacks and restrictions. Keeping digital diplomatic lines private and secure is a major problem. Virtual embassies must have strong cybersecurity measures to safeguard sensitive data and thwart unwanted access as cyber threats continue to emerge. Initiatives for virtual embassies are further hindered by the digital divide since not all populations have equal access to the internet and other digital technology. This restriction hinders inclusion and can exclude certain groups from participating in diplomatic activities.

For international relations, the emergence of virtual embassies and digital diplomacy has important ramifications. First of all, technology may democratize diplomacy by giving nations of all sizes a forum to participate in international affairs. Smaller countries, non-state actors, and marginalized groups may use virtual embassies to increase their visibility, shape global agendas, and take part in diplomatic discussions. Second, virtual embassies might alter how power is distributed in international interactions. Online platforms may enable people and civil society groups to pressure governments, refute myths, and promote social fairness, democracy, and human rights.

Virtual embassies have a bright future in influencing digital diplomacy. Virtual embassies may use artificial intelligence, virtual reality, and augmented reality to improve diplomatic encounters as technology develops. Immersive virtual settings may be used to simulate the experience of visiting a real embassy, letting guests engage with ambassadors, go to virtual events, and discover cultural sites. Furthermore, virtual embassies may work with digital firms and start-ups to provide original solutions for diplomatic problems, promoting innovation and effectiveness in diplomatic procedures.

In the world of digital diplomacy, virtual embassies have become a transformational force. They encourage cultural exchange, boost international ties, and ease diplomatic communication using online platforms and digital technology. Although virtual embassies have many benefits, they also have accessibility and cybersecurity issues. Virtual embassies have the ability to democratize diplomacy and empower a variety of players, which has significant consequences for international relations. Virtual embassies have bright potential for the future, as technological improvements are opening up new channels for diplomatic communication. By taking advantage of the possibilities offered by virtual embassies, countries may reshape digital diplomacy and create stronger, more inclusive international partnerships.

Chapter 4

Social Media and Diplomatic Communication

4. Introduction

Social media platforms have completely changed how people and organizations communicate, and this influence goes beyond just one-on-one encounters. Social media has grown to play a bigger role in diplomatic communication in recent years. Previously carried out behind closed doors and via formal channels, diplomacy has now entered the internet sphere. In this article, the impact of social media on diplomatic communication is investigated, along with the benefits, drawbacks, and possible effects on international relations. We may learn more about how diplomacy is changing in the social media era by examining case studies and talking about pertinent theoretical frameworks.

Diplomats have a rare chance to interact with large worldwide audiences on social media sites like Facebook, Twitter, and Instagram. Social media has proven to be the perfect tool for public diplomacy, which aims to influence public opinion overseas. These channels are being used more often by diplomatic missions and ambassadors to exchange information, advance national interests, and improve a nation's reputation abroad.

Real-time communication made possible by social media allows for the dissolution of geographical boundaries and immediate interaction between diplomats and stakeholders. Platforms like Twitter provide direct and unfiltered communication, allowing diplomats to communicate with people, media, and other diplomats in real-time as well as react to emergencies. This instantaneity of communication has the power to mold narratives and affect how the general public feels about foreign issues.

Social media platforms provide a previously unheard-of degree of accessibility and openness to diplomatic actions. Diplomats may tell the public about their projects, foreign policy, and activities via frequent updates and posts. This openness enhances responsibility, promotes trust, and gives people a voice in the diplomatic process.

Bypassing conventional middlemen, social media enables ambassadors to interact directly with people and stakeholders. A feeling of connection and understanding between diplomatic missions and their target audiences is fostered by this direct involvement, which enables diplomats to obtain information, handle issues, and develop connections. Diplomats may close gaps, clarify myths, and promote trust by participating in public diplomacy operations.

Social media offers a platform for quick and efficient communication during emergencies. Diplomats are able to quickly communicate information, make remarks, and react to developing situations. Using social media channels, ambassadors may dispel rumors, reassure people, and plan rapid international reactions. When resolving international issues and sustaining diplomatic ties, crisis communication agility is essential.

The growth of social media has also created problems with false and misleading information. Information spread quickly and widely on these platforms, which may fuel false narratives and cause misunderstandings or conflicts between nations. Diplomats must use caution while confirming sources, battling erroneous information, and handling any possible consequences.

Social media offers a forum for diplomacy, but it also has inherent security and control problems. Diplomats must walk a tight line between being approachable and safeguarding confidential information. Threats to cybersecurity, hacking attempts, and illegal access to accounts may jeopardize national security and impair diplomatic operations. Strong rules must be put in place by diplomatic missions to protect their online presence.

Despite the benefits, there might be risks associated with relying too much on social media for diplomatic communication. The development of subtle comprehension, empathy, and trust may be hampered by a lack of face-to-face communication and nonverbal indicators. To preserve the depth of traditional diplomacy, diplomatic missions must find a balance between online and offline activities.

The Arab Spring upheavals in the early 2010s brought to light the social media's transforming influence on diplomatic responses. Social media platforms were used by diplomatic missions, international organizations, and activists to organize support, coordinate actions, and overthrow tyrannical governments. This case study serves as an example of how social media may spur diplomatic action and affect political results.

The COVID-19 epidemic forced a change in diplomatic communication, with virtual engagements taking the place of in-person meetings and conventional diplomacy. Social media was essential in enabling distant diplomacy and allowing ambassadors to carry out their duties in spite of travel constraints. The case study of digital diplomacy during the epidemic demonstrates how social media may be flexible in emergency situations.

Diplomats must modify their strategy as social media platforms continue to develop. By offering immersive and engaging experiences, emerging technologies like virtual reality and augmented reality have the potential to improve diplomatic communication even further. The improvements should be tracked by diplomatic missions so they may incorporate them into their digital diplomacy strategies.

Due to the rising use of social media in diplomatic communication, ethical concerns must be carefully considered. Diplomats are expected to act in a professional manner, observe diplomatic conventions, and uphold the fundamentals of international law. Ethics also extends to social media sites' responsibilities for preventing false information, safeguarding user information, and promoting a secure online environment.

Without a doubt, social media has changed how diplomats communicate, offering both possibilities and difficulties. Its ability to promote openness, ease crisis communication, and immediately link ambassadors with global audiences cannot be overstated. However, disinformation, a lack of control, and an overreliance on online connections present vulnerabilities that diplomats must negotiate. Diplomatic missions may adapt to the changing nature of international relations and successfully communicate with a variety of stakeholders in the digital age by using the possibilities of social media while tackling these issues.

4.1 Analyzing the transformative power of social media in diplomatic communication

In today's world, social media has become a potent weapon that has transformed many facets of communication, including diplomatic contacts. Diplomats and other government representatives have recently come to understand the potential of social media platforms to interact with international audiences, convey information, influence public opinion, and even settle disputes. The goal of this article is to examine the transformational potential of social media in diplomatic communication, including the possibilities and problems it brings. We can learn a great deal about the function and importance of social media in influencing international relations by examining case studies and the changing environment of digital diplomacy.

The basis of international relations is diplomatic communication, which involves information exchange, negotiation, and cooperation between countries and diplomats. Traditionally, this communication took place through official channels like diplomatic cables, press releases, and face-to-face encounters. The introduction of social media, however, has given diplomatic communication a new dimension by providing a platform for immediate, interactive, and direct connection with audiences throughout the world.

The way diplomats interact has changed drastically as a result of the social media platforms like Twitter, Facebook, and Instagram expanding so quickly. The large audience that may be reached by diplomats via these channels includes international residents, civil society groups, and even fellow diplomats. Now, diplomats may express their opinions, advance the interests of their nations, and provide real-time information on developments in discussions and events. Diplomats now have a more direct and uncensored voice in international affairs due to their ability to circumvent conventional media gatekeepers.

It is crucial to look at noteworthy case studies that show the influence of social media in diplomatic communication in order to comprehend its revolutionary capacity. One such instance is the Arab Spring, during which social media significantly contributed to public mobilization, information dissemination, and political change in the Middle East and North Africa. Governments also actively use social media for public diplomacy, as seen by the United States State Department's Twitter account's strategic communication efforts and other countries' digital diplomacy programs.

While there are many potential for diplomatic engagement on social media, there are also hazards and difficulties that diplomats must manage. The dissemination of false information, the inability to control narratives, and the possibility of diplomatic blunders and errors all provide new challenges for diplomats. Additionally, the need for immediate replies and the possibility of information overload may tax diplomatic resources and raise the danger of mistakes or misunderstandings. To reduce these hazards and guarantee appropriate and efficient use of social media platforms, diplomats must adopt policies.

Despite these obstacles, social media has enormous advantages and prospects for diplomatic communication. Bypassing conventional media filters and magnifying diplomatic messages, it offers a forum for communicating directly with people. Social media technologies help track II diplomacy by enabling citizens, civil society groups, and non-governmental players to participate in diplomatic conversations and efforts. Additionally, social media may build more inclusive and democratic diplomatic procedures by encouraging openness, accountability, and public involvement.

Social media sites have the ability to aid in dispute resolution by fostering communication and mutual understanding between the parties. Social media's ability to humanize disputes and highlight many viewpoints might aid in bridging gaps and increasing empathy. By using social media to interact with stakeholders and resolve conflicts, diplomats may facilitate discussions and foster confidence. However, it's important to take into account the dangers of social media being used for provocation and propaganda.

It is crucial to look at future trends and their consequences for diplomatic communication as social media continues to change. The future of digital diplomacy will be shaped by the emergence of new platforms like TikTok and Clubhouse as well as the incorporation of cutting-edge technology like virtual reality and artificial intelligence. Understanding these patterns may help policymakers and diplomats prepare for future possibilities and challenges, allowing them to successfully adapt and capitalize on social media's revolutionary impact.

Diplomats now have new channels for participation, information sharing, and dispute resolution thanks to social media, which has emerged as a revolutionary force in diplomatic communication. Despite the dangers and obstacles it poses, there are more advantages and possibilities. Diplomats must change with the times and recognize the power of social media in influencing world affairs. Diplomats may promote more inclusive, transparent, and successful diplomatic procedures in the digital age by using the transformational potential of social media.

4.2 Case studies highlighting successful social media campaigns by diplomatic actors

The ability of social media platforms to influence public opinion, advance foreign policy goals, and interact with a global audience has become more apparent to diplomatic players throughout the globe. This essay intends to investigate and evaluate a number of case studies that showcase effective social media campaigns run by diplomatic actors. We may learn a lot about the methods, tactics, and effects of these campaigns by looking at these instances, which will help us understand how successful they are at attaining diplomatic objectives.

The "Digital Outreach Team" of the U.S. State Department is a great illustration of a diplomatic actor's effective social media campaign. The group interacts with international audiences in real-time through websites like Facebook, Twitter, and YouTube, dispelling false information, offering factual information, and advancing American principles. The Digital Outreach Team has successfully changed public opinion and cultivated connections with people in target locations by taking a proactive approach to social media diplomacy, supporting American foreign policy goals.

The "Indiafrica" campaign from the Indian Ministry of External Affairs is a prime example of how social media may be used to strengthen diplomatic connections with African countries. The campaign used social media outlets like Instagram and Twitter to highlight the common history, culture, and ambitions between India and Africa. Audiences all throughout the continent were moved by the campaign's creative mix of narrative, visual material, and interactive components, which improved ties between nations and encouraged collaboration.

The Swedish Institute launched the "Curators of Sweden" initiative in an effort to empower everyday Swedes to influence how the nation is seen online. The effort offered a genuine and varied viewpoint on Swedish culture, beliefs, and politics by turning over control of the official Twitter account to a new person each week. The effort attracted a lot of interest and participation, demonstrating Sweden as an open, democratic, and welcoming country while effectively advancing diplomatic goals.

Social media was used by the South Korean Ministry of Foreign Affairs' "New Horizons" campaign to promote Korean culture and raise the nation's international profile. The campaign featured Korean entertainment, fashion, technology, and food via channels like YouTube, aiming to appeal to youthful people throughout the globe. The program effectively enhanced favorable opinions of South Korea and drew foreign tourists by capitalizing on the appeal of Korean popular culture, enhancing the nation's soft power and diplomatic outreach.

The "Alliance in Action" campaign from the Canadian Embassy in Washington, D.C. is an example of how social media may be used to include both home and foreign audiences in diplomatic conversations. The campaign included virtual town hall meetings, expert panels, and online conversations on subjects including trade and security using channels like Facebook Live and Twitter.

The program promoted openness, inclusiveness, and public involvement by using digital channels for public diplomacy, enhancing Canada's diplomatic ties.

An example of how social media may be used to counter false information and promote trustworthy information during emergencies is the United Nations' "Verified" campaign. The campaign sought to stop the spread of incorrect information about the COVID-19 epidemic via collaborations with influencers and social media platforms. During the time of the global health crisis, the campaign was essential in influencing public opinion and promoting responsible behavior by dispelling misconceptions, disseminating correct information, and amplifying reliable sources.

The case studies included in this article show how effective social media campaigns can be in advancing diplomatic goals. Diplomatic actors have used social media platforms to forge connections, sway public opinion, and accomplish foreign policy objectives, from combating disinformation to fostering cultural exchange and boosting public involvement. These campaigns have successfully used social media as a diplomatic instrument by adopting cutting-edge tactics, using visual and interactive material, and interacting with a variety of audiences. It is crucial for diplomatic players to adjust and take use of social media's potential for successful engagement and communication in order to support the development of a more connected and informed global community.

4.3 Navigating the challenges of diplomacy in the age of viral content and disinformation

Due to the spread of viral material and misinformation, diplomacy confronts unprecedented hurdles in today's linked world. With the growth of social media and digital platforms, there are now new ways for viral material and misinformation to influence public opinion and thwart diplomatic efforts. The goal of this article is to examine the many difficulties that diplomats confront while navigating this environment and to provide solutions.

In the context of diplomacy, the influence of viral material cannot be understated. Social media platforms make it possible for information to spread quickly, enabling messages, photographs, and videos to instantly reach millions of people. The power to become viral presents diplomatic possibilities as well as difficulties. On the one hand, viral material may help with diplomatic project marketing and help win over the public. On the other side, technology may also disseminate false information and warp public opinion, making diplomatic attempts more difficult. To take advantage of viral content's beneficial potential while minimizing its negative effects, diplomats must negotiate these dynamics.

Diplomacy is seriously threatened by disinformation, which is purposeful misinformation disseminated with the intention of misleading. Digital platforms are used by both state and non-state actors to spread misinformation campaigns that try to sway public opinion and affect diplomatic results. Disinformation erodes international confidence, escalates tensions, and obstructs productive communication. To protect the credibility of diplomatic procedures and sustain fruitful relationships, diplomats must be skilled at spotting and dispelling false information.

In the era of viral material and misinformation, digital diplomacy has become an essential instrument for diplomats. Diplomats may interact directly with audiences throughout the globe by using social media and digital platforms, circumventing conventional media gatekeepers. Diplomats may influence narratives, combat misinformation, and increase public support for their projects via the use of digital diplomacy. Diplomats, however, have difficulties while using internet platforms, including maintaining online identities, safeguarding private data, and assuring authenticity in the face of many bogus accounts and automated bots.

Diplomats must use a multifaceted strategy to develop resilience in order to successfully negotiate the difficulties of misinformation. This entails creating collaborations with internet businesses to combat misinformation at its source, encouraging fact-checking projects, and improving media literacy and critical thinking among the general public. Additionally, ambassadors need to work together worldwide to create standards and guidelines that combat misinformation while upholding the right to free expression and information. Diplomats may lessen the damaging effects of misinformation and sustain public confidence in diplomatic procedures by strengthening their resistance to it.

Effective diplomatic communication is essential in the era of viral material and misinformation. In order to successfully engage audiences and cut through the clutter, diplomats must modify their communication tactics. Utilizing compelling tales that connect with the target audience, visual material, and storytelling approaches are necessary for this. To combat misinformation and foster trust, diplomacy must be open, understandable, and approachable. To further magnify their thoughts and reach bigger audiences, diplomats should collaborate with conventional media, civil society groups, and internet influencers.

Technology advancements provide diplomats useful tools to combat the problems caused by viral material and misinformation. Machine learning algorithms and artificial intelligence (AI) may be used to monitor sentiment, spot patterns of misinformation, and determine the effect of viral material. Blockchain technology also shows promise for boosting the reliability of online communication channels and authenticating content. To fully realize the potential of these technology solutions for diplomatic success, diplomats should investigate them and collaborate closely with specialists.

Diplomats need specific training and programs to improve their ability if they are to successfully traverse the difficulties of diplomacy in the era of viral material and misinformation. Media literacy, digital diplomacy, and debunking misinformation should all be taught at diplomacy academies and institutions. Additionally, diplomats should actively participate in lifelong learning by going to conferences and seminars on new trends and tactics. Diplomatic operations might be better equipped to traverse the changing digital terrain by providing diplomats with the required training and information.

In the era of misinformation and viral material, diplomacy has new problems. The influence of viral content and the widespread spread of misinformation hamper diplomatic efforts and erode international confidence. However, diplomats may successfully manage these difficulties by embracing digital diplomacy, developing resilience against misinformation, bolstering communication tactics, using technology, and investing in training and capacity development. In order to conduct successful diplomacy in the face of viral material and misinformation, diplomats must adapt to the rapidly changing digital world, take use of its potential, and establish new avenues.

Chapter 5

Cybersecurity and Digital Diplomacy

5. Introduction

Cybersecurity has grown to be a major worry for all levels of society in the age of fast digital change. Because of how linked our contemporary world is, there are now a wide variety of cyberthreats, from identity theft and data breaches to state-sponsored cyberespionage and hostile assaults on vital infrastructure. In order to preserve their national interests and promote collaboration on cybersecurity concerns, governments must traverse the complexity of cyberspace. As a result, the area of digital diplomacy has become a crucial part of international relations. This article examines the complex interrelationship between cybersecurity and digital diplomacy, looking at the difficulties, possibilities, and tactics used by governments to protect their interests and conduct effective diplomacy online.

The term "cybersecurity" describes the precautions taken to guard against unwanted access, interruption, and damage to computer systems, networks, and data. Because of the rapid development of digital technology, cybersecurity is becoming a major problem on a worldwide scale. Malicious actors, such as state-sponsored hackers, criminal gangs, and hacktivists, are always looking for ways to attack weak points in cyberspace. Therefore, to protect their vital infrastructure, secure sensitive data, and guarantee the integrity of their digital systems, governments must implement strong cybersecurity frameworks.

The practice of using digital tools and platforms to perform diplomatic operations, encourage international collaboration, and advance a nation's foreign policy goals is referred to as digital diplomacy, sometimes known as e-diplomacy or cyber diplomacy. Digital diplomacy is integrated with conventional diplomatic tactics in today's linked society. Governments may use it to participate in public diplomacy initiatives, speak with international audiences directly, and tackle world problems online.

Challenges to Cybersecurity in the Field of Digital Diplomacy:

a. State-Sponsored Cyber Espionage: Nation-states often use cyber espionage to obtain information, keep tabs on other nations' operations, and gain an advantage over rivals. Such actions may undermine diplomatic connections and erode international confidence. To protect national security interests, digital diplomacy must consider the ongoing danger of state-sponsored cyberattacks and build strong defenses.

b. Malware and Ransomware assaults: Criminals target government networks with malware and ransomware assaults to steal sensitive data. These assaults have the potential to sabotage diplomatic communications, jeopardize private discussions, and harm reputations. For the purpose of reducing the danger of such attacks and ensuring the continuation of diplomatic activities, diplomatic missions must prioritize cybersecurity measures.

c. Influence operations and disinformation: Disinformation campaigns, influence operations, and the spread of false news are all flourishing in the digital sphere. Social media platforms are used by both state and non-state actors to sway public opinion, foment strife, and thwart diplomatic attempts. Governments must create methods to combat misinformation and increase their capacity to withstand these internet dangers.

Digital Diplomacy Techniques to Improve Cybersecurity:

a. International collaboration: In order to promote international collaboration, countries should participate in multilateral forums given the transnational character of cybersecurity concerns. Collaboration efforts may encourage knowledge exchange, capacity growth, and the creation of universal rules and standards in cyberspace.

b. Public-private partnerships: Public-private partnerships may be established between governments and businesses in the private sector to improve cybersecurity measures. Collaboration with IT companies, cybersecurity businesses, and academic institutions may speed up information sharing, collaborative research, and the creation of cutting-edge countermeasures to cyberthreats.

c. Engagement in Diplomacy and the Development of Norms: Digital diplomacy offers a forum for diplomatic engagement on cybersecurity challenges. Governments may debate standards, guidelines, and responsible state conduct in cyberspace via bilateral and international diplomatic channels. Norm-building initiatives may assist in establishing standards for ethical behavior and lowering the likelihood of cyber confrontations.

d. Building cybersecurity capabilities: Building cybersecurity capabilities should be a top priority for governments both locally and globally. A nation's capacity to avoid, recognize, and react to cyber threats may be improved through investing in education, training programs, and skill development. Supporting capacity-building programs in underdeveloped nations may also increase the resilience of the global cybersecurity ecosystem.

e. Incident response and crisis management: Despite effective preventative measures, cybersecurity events are unavoidable. To lessen the effects of cyberattacks, governments must create efficient incident response and crisis management procedures. Plans for coordination, information sharing, and open lines of communication with pertinent parties should all be included.

Cybersecurity and digital diplomacy are intricately interwoven in the connected digital world. To safeguard their national interests and successfully participate in digital diplomacy, governments must understand the significance of strong cybersecurity measures. Countries may negotiate the complexity of cyberspace and guarantee the security and stability of the digital sphere by tackling the issues presented by cyber threats, using international collaboration, and adopting proactive tactics. In order to create a safe and prosperous future in the era of digital transformation, a comprehensive strategy that integrates cybersecurity and digital diplomacy will be essential.

5.1 Investigating the importance of cybersecurity in the practice of digital diplomacy

For countries to participate in international relations, communication, and negotiation, digital diplomacy has become an essential instrument. Governments all around the globe have adopted digital platforms to conduct diplomatic operations, improve diplomatic relations, and advance their national interests in response to the fast growth of technology. However, the susceptibility to cyber assaults increases as the dependence on digital infrastructure increases. Cybersecurity becomes crucial in the conduct of digital diplomacy in this situation. In order to better understand cybersecurity's role in digital diplomacy, this article will examine its significance, issues, and possible solutions.

The first part gives an outline of how digital diplomacy has developed, focusing on how technology has changed conventional diplomatic procedures. It looks at how social media, online platforms, and other technological advancements have made it possible for governments to interact with overseas audiences, disseminate information, and influence public opinion. Because of the potential and difficulties brought on by our dependence on digital technology, cybersecurity is a crucial component of digital diplomacy.

In-depth discussion of cybersecurity and its particular implications for digital diplomacy is provided in this section. It looks at the numerous cyber dangers that nations using digital diplomacy must deal with, including hacking, data breaches, defamation campaigns, and cyber espionage. It highlights the negative effects that might result from these risks, such as weakened national security, strained diplomatic ties, and declining public confidence. Policymakers may better comprehend the need for effective cybersecurity measures by being aware of the complexity of cybersecurity concerns.

The article examines the value of cybersecurity in the use of digital diplomacy in this part. It explores the function of cybersecurity in preserving vital infrastructure, guaranteeing the integrity of data transferred between countries, and protecting private diplomatic conversations. The effects of cyber events on diplomatic discussions, global reputation, and foreign policy goals are also covered. The section emphasizes the crucial relevance of cybersecurity as a basis for efficient and safe digital diplomacy by emphasizing these issues.

In the practice of digital diplomacy, cybersecurity presents a number of difficulties and complexity. It talks on the asymmetrical nature of cyberwarfare, the dynamic nature of cyberthreats, and the challenges of attribution in cyberspace. It also looks at the difficulties associated with international collaboration, information exchange, and international policy coordination. In order to successfully combat evolving threats, the section highlights the necessity for adaptable and proactive methods to cybersecurity.

This part examines various methods for enhancing cybersecurity in digital diplomacy, building on the issues covered in the preceding section. It looks at the significance of creating thorough cybersecurity frameworks, encouraging global collaboration and information sharing, boosting technological capabilities, and spending money on cyber education and awareness. The importance of public-private collaborations in solving cybersecurity issues and promoting innovation is also highlighted in this section.

The case studies and best practices presented in this section illustrate effective cybersecurity strategies used in digital diplomacy. The analysis highlights the methods, policies, and results of some countries that have successfully included cybersecurity into their diplomatic procedures. The case studies provide useful information and lessons that may help practitioners and policymakers improve cybersecurity protocols and construct robust frameworks for digital diplomacy.

The summary of the essay's main results in the last part emphasizes the significance of cybersecurity in the use of digital diplomacy. It highlights the necessity for proactive and all-encompassing cybersecurity tactics to reduce risks, safeguard private data, and defend diplomatic goals. In order to confront the changing cybersecurity environment, the article emphasizes the value of international collaboration, policy coordination, and adaptive measures. Nations can guarantee the efficacy, integrity, and trust of their digital diplomatic activities in the digital age by giving cybersecurity first priority.

5.2 Exploring the role of cybersecurity in safeguarding diplomatic networks and data

The importance of cybersecurity in protecting diplomatic networks and data has grown more important than ever in today's linked world, where digital communication has become a major component of diplomatic operations. The foundation of international relations, diplomatic networks, which include embassies, consulates, and other official missions, aid in intergovernmental coordination and communication. These networks are, however, very susceptible to cyberthreats including hacking, espionage, and data breaches. The goal of this article is to examine the value of cybersecurity in defending diplomatic networks and data, with a focus on the difficulties and techniques involved in reducing cyber threats.

The main method of communication for diplomatic missions is via diplomatic networks. These networks make it possible to send private conversations, diplomatic cables, and other sensitive material in a secure manner. Such data breaches may have far-reaching repercussions, endangering international ties, imperiling diplomatic discussions, and endangering national security. Given how vital these networks are, protecting them from online attacks is of utmost significance.

Due to their high-value targets and the constantly changing nature of cyber attacks, diplomatic networks confront a number of cybersecurity issues. Hackers, state-sponsored actors, and cybercriminals regularly take advantage of holes in network architecture, software, and user behavior to enter diplomatic networks without authorization. Diplomatic systems are often compromised via social engineering methods, malware infestations, and phishing attempts. Additionally, as internet of things (IoT) devices and cloud-based services are being used by diplomatic missions, the attack surface is expanded and strong cybersecurity measures are required.

Comprehensive cybersecurity solutions must be adopted to protect diplomatic networks. The multi-layered strategy that these tactics should use includes technology controls, policy frameworks, and human awareness. In order to stop unwanted access and harmful activity, strong perimeter defenses must be in place. These defenses should include firewalls, intrusion detection systems, and secure gateways. Regular penetration tests and vulnerability assessments may help find and fix flaws in the network architecture.

Data security techniques should be used to protect data both in transit and at rest. For diplomats working remotely or gaining access to sensitive information from faraway areas, secure communication channels may be provided using virtual private networks (VPNs) and secure sockets layer (SSL) certificates. Sensitive data exposure may be restricted and only authorized people can access certain data sets thanks to data loss prevention (DLP) technologies and access control regulations.

Furthermore, it is essential for diplomatic missions to have a strong incident response strategy. Rapid cyber incident identification and reaction may lessen the effects and stop additional network and data intrusion. To guarantee data accessibility in the case of a breach or system failure, regular backup and disaster recovery protocols should also be put in place.

Successful cyberattacks may be thwarted by diplomatic posts having a robust cybersecurity culture. The best practices for safe communication, the most recent cyberthreats, and awareness programs for diplomatic workers should all be provided on a regular basis. The significance of using strong passwords, two-factor authentication, and being careful while handling email attachments and links are some examples of this.

Cooperation and information exchange between diplomatic missions are essential for improving cybersecurity. Diplomats may keep ahead of new cyber risks by exchanging threat information, best practices, and lessons learned. Such collaboration is facilitated by international organizations and institutions like the United Nations and Interpol, which provide venues for knowledge sharing and capacity development.

To improve their cybersecurity posture, diplomatic missions must interact with the business sector. Private cybersecurity firms are equipped with the technical knowledge and resources to help provide tailored security solutions for diplomatic networks. Public-private collaborations may promote sophisticated cybersecurity technology innovation, research, and development, ensuring that diplomatic missions are prepared to successfully confront new threats.

Ensuring the cybersecurity of diplomatic networks and data is essential as the digital world develops. Strong cybersecurity policies that include technological controls, regulatory frameworks, and human awareness must be prioritized by diplomatic missions. Diplomatic networks may bolster their defenses and safeguard critical information from cyber attacks by investing in cutting-edge technology, promoting a cybersecurity culture, and developing engagement with the private sector and international organizations. In addition to being essential for sustaining international confidence, stability, and efficient diplomacy, protecting diplomatic networks is also important for national security.

5.3 Addressing the challenges of cyber threats and international cooperation in the digital realm

The widespread use of digital technology in today's linked society has completely changed many facets of our daily lives. The digital world provides a wide range of advantages, but there has also been an alarming rise in cyber risks. The security and stability of countries, organizations, and people are seriously threatened by these dangers. To overcome these obstacles, strong international collaboration and coordinated efforts are needed to create efficient policies, structures, and processes to reduce cyber hazards. The complexity of cyberthreats, the need of international collaboration, and the steps that may be done to successfully tackle these difficulties will all be covered in this article.

Cyber threats include a variety of harmful actions carried out over digital networks that threaten infrastructure, data, and computer systems. These dangers take many different forms, such as ransomware, malware, phishing assaults, and state-sponsored cyberespionage. These dangers have an effect that is not limited to a single country; they have the potential to inflict significant disruption and economic losses on a global scale. Making effective countermeasures against cyber threats requires an understanding of their nature, extent, and effects.

Cyber dangers are transnational and sophisticated, necessitating coordinated worldwide action to successfully combat them. To exchange information, intelligence, and best practices, cooperation is essential across countries, governments, law enforcement agencies, and business sector organizations. International collaboration may encourage information sharing, collective defense, and the creation of sound digital standards and legal frameworks. Nations may improve their ability to avoid, identify, and quickly and effectively react to cyber attacks by collaborating.

Despite the crucial relevance of global cooperation in combating cyber threats, a number of obstacles prevent efficient cooperation. One major obstacle is the absence of uniform laws and legal systems between countries, which makes it difficult to prosecute hackers operating out of countries with lax cybersecurity regulations. Information exchange between nations is often hampered by sovereignty difficulties and national security concerns. Furthermore, forging comprehensive cooperation agreements is complicated by divergent geopolitical interests and low levels of international trust.

There are numerous actions that may be made to encourage global digital collaboration. First, the creation of universal standards and guidelines for state conduct in cyberspace may serve as a basis for collaboration. Mutual trust may be promoted while lowering the likelihood of cyber warfare by enforcing these principles between states. Second, the establishment of international forums or organizations devoted to cybersecurity may promote international communication, information sharing, and cooperation. To improve collaboration, existing efforts like the Global Forum on Cyber Expertise (GFCE) and the United Nations Group of Governmental Experts (UN GGE) may be developed and extended.

Effective international collaboration requires that governments, especially those with limited resources, improve their cybersecurity capabilities. Initiatives to enhance national capacity in cybersecurity might concentrate on providing technical support, training courses, and knowledge-sharing forums to aid in the establishment of Computer Emergency Response Teams (CERTs) and strong cybersecurity frameworks. Through money, advice, and technology transfer, developed countries may contribute significantly to capacity development initiatives, promoting a more secure global digital environment.

Dealing with cyber dangers and enhancing international collaboration need including the corporate sector. Private businesses have tremendous knowledge, assets, and technology breakthroughs that may help fight cyber threats. Public-private partnerships may make it easier for people to share information, conduct collaborative research and development, and create industry standards. Collaboration across public, business, and academic institutions may lead to the creation of novel approaches, early detection systems, and more potent incident response tools.

To counteract cyber risks, comprehensive legal and regulatory frameworks must be developed at the national and international levels. Nations should pass legislation that makes cybercrime illegal, enables international collaboration in investigations, and creates means for extraditing cyberterrorists. Additionally, the creation of international conventions and treaties helps reconcile legal systems and promote successful international collaboration. A famous example of such a convention is the Budapest Convention on Cybercrime, which offers a framework for collaboration and standardization of cybercrime laws.

A fundamental idea in combating cyberthreats and promoting global collaboration is multistakeholderism, which includes the involvement of governments, businesses, civil society groups, and academics. A balanced and inclusive approach may be ensured by include a variety of stakeholders in the processes of policymaking, standard-setting, and implementation. This method may assist in addressing the worries and viewpoints of all relevant stakeholders and help develop more practical and universally acceptable responses to cyber risks.

The difficulties posed by cyber attacks in the digital sphere call for strong international collaboration. Nations may improve their cybersecurity capabilities, exchange knowledge and best practices, and create thorough legal and legislative frameworks by acknowledging the interrelated nature of the threats and actively participating in joint initiatives. The international community can create a safe and resilient digital environment via capacity building, public-private partnerships, and multistakeholder engagement, reducing the dangers presented by cyberthreats and guaranteeing the sustainable growth and prosperity of countries in the digital era.

Chapter 6

E-Diplomacy and International Negotiations

6. Introduction

E-diplomacy, commonly referred to as digital diplomacy or diplomacy 2.0, describes how diplomacy and international talks are conducted using digital platforms and technology. Traditional diplomatic procedures have evolved to include digital tools and tactics as the globe becomes more linked and technology-driven. This change has significantly improved the effectiveness, accessibility, and scope of international discussions. We shall discuss the idea of e-diplomacy and its consequences for international negotiations in this article.

Since the earliest human civilizations, diplomacy has played a significant role in human history. Negotiations, document exchanges, and face-to-face meetings between ambassadors were all part of traditional diplomacy. Technology has changed diplomacy and made it possible for diplomats to interact and communicate with their colleagues from a distance. E-diplomacy is a result of the internet and other digital technologies' revolutionary change on how diplomats work.

E-diplomacy uses a variety of online resources and platforms to speed up diplomatic procedures. Email, video conferencing, social networking, virtual collaboration tools, and encrypted communication routes are some of these resources. Diplomats may now interact with a broader audience via social media platforms, communicate instantaneously across time zones, and exchange papers online. E-diplomacy has improved the effectiveness, openness, and accessibility of diplomacy.

International discussions may benefit from e-diplomacy in a number of ways. First of all, it enables real-time communication, allowing diplomats to have an instant conversation and quickly share information. This quickness and effectiveness may hasten dispute resolution and the negotiating process. Second, e-diplomacy improves accessibility by removing the need for physical presence, which lowers travel expenses and logistical difficulties. From their home nations, diplomats may take part in discussions, providing a more inclusive and varied representation. Thirdly, digital platforms make it possible for a wider range of stakeholders to participate in the negotiating process, including members of civil society groups, non-governmental actors, and ordinary people. This inclusion encourages legitimacy and openness in cross-border talks.

E-diplomacy has many benefits, but there are drawbacks as well. The digital gap is a significant issue since not all nations and people have equal access to technology and the internet. This gap in access has the potential to skew discussions and prevent the involvement of voices from the margins. Additionally, cyber risks such as hacking, espionage, and defamation campaigns may affect the digital world. In order to protect the integrity and secrecy of their communications, diplomats must negotiate these security concerns. The use of digital tools also raises questions about data privacy and security since sensitive information given during talks may be intercepted or used improperly.

In several international discussions and diplomatic procedures, e-diplomacy has been widely employed. For instance, it has been essential in the discussions on climate change, as diplomats from various nations work remotely to create and carry out climate policy. The usage of digital platforms has made it possible to share, coordinate, and keep track of developments in real time. E-diplomacy has also proved helpful in attempts to resolve conflicts, such peace talks and discussions for a cease-fire. Even in the absence of physical contact, virtual diplomacy allows for communication between disputing parties, fostering de-escalation and reconciliation.

The idea of "soft power," which refers to a nation's capacity to influence others via persuasion, culture, and ideals rather than coercion or force, has also been broadened by e-diplomacy. Countries may use digital platforms to project their soft power by presenting their cultural traditions, highlighting their economic advantages, and running public diplomacy initiatives. Twitter and Facebook have developed into crucial instruments for governments to interact directly with residents of other nations, influencing public opinion and fostering partnerships.

E-diplomacy will probably see future changes as technology develops. Language translation, data analysis, and decision assistance might all be automated as a result of the development of artificial intelligence (AI) and machine learning (ML). However, when using AI in diplomacy, officials must carefully evaluate the moral ramifications and possible biases. Diplomats could also be able to participate in immersive virtual meetings and simulations as virtual reality (VR) and augmented reality (AR) technology develop, improving the negotiating process.

Diplomats are now able to communicate, negotiate, and work together more effectively and fairly because to e-diplomacy, which has evolved as a crucial part of international talks. With real-time communication, more stakeholder participation, and improved accessibility, digital tools and platforms have changed diplomatic procedures. E-diplomacy has advantages in terms of speed, inclusiveness, and openness, but it also has drawbacks including the digital gap and cybersecurity dangers. E-diplomacy will continue to influence future international discussions as technology develops, enabling a more connected and effective diplomatic scene.

6.1 Unpacking the role of e-diplomacy in international negotiations and diplomacy

E-diplomacy is the use of information and communication technologies (ICTs) in diplomatic actions and international talks. It is sometimes referred to as digital diplomacy or diplomacy in the digital age. E-diplomacy has become a vital instrument for diplomats and negotiators to improve their efficacy and efficiency in solving global difficulties as a result of the fast improvements in technology. In order to better understand the role of e-diplomacy in international negotiations and diplomacy, this article will examine its advantages, disadvantages, and prospective consequences for diplomatic practice in the future.

E-diplomacy is the use of ICTs for diplomatic operations such as representation, negotiation, and communication in the context of international relations. It includes numerous digital technologies that allow diplomats to communicate and engage with stakeholders beyond geographic borders, including email, video conferencing, social media, and virtual platforms.

E-diplomacy's origins may be found in the early days of telegraph and telephone communication. As e-diplomacy has grown over time, the digitization of diplomatic procedures and the introduction of new diplomatic practices have been made possible.

Through real-time communication and the ability to communicate across geographic boundaries, e-diplomacy promotes swift knowledge transfer and information exchange. This speeds up the negotiating process and enhances decision-making, producing diplomatic results that are more effective and efficient.

All participants in international discussions, including historically underrepresented voices, may compete on an even playing field thanks to digital platforms. As a result, the legitimacy and representativeness of diplomatic procedures are strengthened. E-diplomacy contributes to amplifying different viewpoints, enhancing participation, and promoting inclusion.

Electronic diplomacy (e-diplomacy) expands the reach of diplomatic statements beyond conventional channels via social media platforms and online participation. It enables ambassadors to interact directly with audiences throughout the world, influencing public opinion and advancing their nation's foreign policy goals.

The expenditures related to conventional diplomatic activities, such as travel fees and physical infrastructure, are greatly reduced by e-diplomacy. Diplomats may devote resources more effectively and to more urgent issues by using virtual meetings and online discussions to reduce logistical difficulties.

It is difficult to apply e-diplomacy fairly given the disparities in nations and regions in terms of access to technology and dependable internet connection. The digital gap makes already existing disparities worse and prevents everyone from participating fully in international discussions.

The dependence on digital platforms raises questions about cybersecurity and the safeguarding of private data. Due to the possibility of hacking, spying, and unwanted access, diplomatic communications must be protected with strict security measures and diplomatic norms.

A change in diplomatic culture and methods is needed to implement e-diplomacy. By combining the advantages of technology with the need of interpersonal ties and trust-building inherent in conventional diplomatic procedures, diplomats must adjust to new forms of communication and negotiation.

Investment in training and capacity development is required for diplomats to gain the appropriate digital skills as part of the integration of e-diplomacy. To provide diplomats the skills they need for the digital age, diplomatic academies and training centers should include digital literacy and e-diplomacy courses in their curricula.

Governments, non-state entities, and civil society may better collaborate and work together thanks to e-diplomacy. Digital platforms provide forums for discussion and collaboration, facilitating more involvement in international negotiations and encouraging creative responses to societal problems.

The need for new rules and governance frameworks to manage digital diplomacy is called into question by the rising dependence on e-diplomacy. To ensure accountability and transparency in digital diplomatic engagements, diplomatic players must have conversations to create standards for responsible and ethical e-diplomacy activities.

International discussions and diplomacy are being transformed by e-diplomacy. Its advantages, including improved communication, more inclusion, and cost effectiveness, have the power to alter diplomatic procedures and advance more effective global governance. To fully use the advantages of e-diplomacy, issues like the digital divide and security concerns must be addressed. In order to ensure that e-diplomacy is used as a weapon for developing international cooperation and attaining diplomatic goals, it is important to strike a balance between conventional diplomatic rules and the new possibilities afforded by digital technology.

6.2 Examining the use of digital tools for diplomatic negotiations and conflict resolution

With the use of digital instruments, diplomacy and conflict resolution have greatly changed in the contemporary period. The use of digital technology has enhanced and, in some instances, changed conventional conflict resolution and negotiating processes. The different facets of digital technologies used in diplomatic talks and conflict settlement are explored in this article. We may learn more about the usefulness and potential of these instruments in influencing future international relations by studying their advantages, difficulties, and possibilities.

Diplomatic talks were traditionally conducted via in-person meetings, extensive documentation, and the use of middlemen. However, the scene has changed as a result of the development of digital technologies. The negotiating process has been transformed by digital technologies including secure communication platforms, video conferencing, and collaborative software. These techniques allow in-the-moment communication, boost information exchange, and improve the openness, effectiveness, and inclusiveness of negotiations.

A sophisticated approach is necessary for conflict resolution, and digital technologies have been helpful in this area. Online discussion forums, mediation software, and data analytics tools have all been very helpful in fostering communication, examining conflict patterns, and putting forward workable solutions. Processes for resolving disputes have become more accessible, participatory, and potentially impartial thanks to digitalization.

There are various benefits of using digital technologies in diplomatic discussions and conflict settlement. First and foremost, they allow remote participation and remove geographical obstacles, promoting inclusion and diversity in negotiating processes. Second, by recording interactions, disseminating knowledge, and encouraging stakeholder responsibility, these systems improve transparency. Digital technologies also make it possible to gather, analyze, and visualize data effectively, giving diplomats and mediators important information they may use to make wise decisions. Additionally, digital platforms provide private communication and negotiating channels that are secure, protecting critical data.

Although digital instruments have many advantages, they also have drawbacks. The problem of security and trust is one of the main worries. The integrity of digital discussions may be compromised by cybersecurity risks, data breaches, and illegal access. Additionally, the digital gap across nations and regions may result in differences in access to and competence with digital technologies, which can impede inclusive participation. The efficiency of digital discussions may also be impacted by language and cultural hurdles, necessitating careful thought and tool customization for various circumstances.

This section includes case studies that demonstrate the actual use of digital technologies in diplomatic negotiations and conflict settlement. Examples include the use of data analytics to analyze conflict dynamics, the use of video conferencing in peace discussions, and the use of online dispute resolution systems to settle territorial disputes. These case studies emphasize the advantages, difficulties, and lessons discovered while using digital technologies in different diplomatic situations.

The use of digital technologies in diplomatic discussions and conflict resolution seems to have a bright future. Natural language processing, machine learning, and artificial intelligence developments have the ability to improve decision-making, automate tedious operations, and provide real-time translation services. By mimicking actual presence and immersive experiences, the merger of virtual reality and augmented reality technology might further alter the negotiating process. To guarantee the ethical and fair use of developing technologies, governments must address ethical problems, data privacy concerns, and legal frameworks.

The area of international relations has changed as a result of the employment of digital technologies in diplomatic discussions and conflict settlement. The advantages of digital technologies are apparent, despite ongoing difficulties and restrictions. They open up new channels for conversation and conflict resolution while improving efficiency, inclusiveness, transparency, and decision-making in negotiations. Policymakers and practitioners may take use of the promise of digital technologies to promote peace, settle disputes, and create a more linked and collaborative world by embracing technology breakthroughs and tackling accompanying problems.

6.3 Assessing the impact of e-diplomacy on traditional diplomatic practices and protocols

Statecraft has long been based on diplomacy, the art of conducting talks and maintaining international relations. But the development of technology and the growth of the digital age have fundamentally altered how diplomacy is carried out. E-diplomacy has arisen as a revolutionary force in the development of diplomatic practices and norms. It includes the use of digital tools and platforms in diplomatic activity. This article seeks to evaluate how e-diplomacy affects conventional diplomatic procedures and norms by looking at its benefits, drawbacks, and possible future effects.

E-diplomacy has transformed conventional diplomatic procedures thanks to its many benefits. First of all, it has improved dialogue and information exchange between diplomats and decision-makers. Diplomats may connect and share information in real-time across geographical boundaries by using email, instant messaging services, and video conferencing. This speeds up the decision-making process and makes it easier to react quickly to changing circumstances.

Second, the reach and breadth of diplomacy have increased as a result of e-diplomacy. Diplomats may interact directly with individuals on social media sites like Twitter and Facebook, supporting public diplomacy projects. Digital platforms also make it possible to hold summits and meetings virtually, which increases participation and lowers the expense of physical travel. This inclusiveness improves openness and makes it easier for many viewpoints to be represented in diplomatic procedures.

Despite its benefits, e-diplomacy presents serious obstacles to established diplomatic conventions and procedures. The digital gap, which refers to states' uneven access to technology and digital resources, is one of the main issues. Developing nations and disadvantaged groups could be excluded from diplomatic procedures because they lack the facilities and expertise required to effectively engage in e-diplomacy. It becomes essential to address this gap if inclusive and fair diplomacy is to be achieved.

The deterioration of diplomatic secrecy and privacy is another issue. The danger of cyberthreats and data breaches increases with the rising dependence on digital communication methods. Concerns about the security and integrity of diplomatic contacts are raised by the possibility of intercepting or compromising critical talks and diplomatic correspondence. As a result, it is necessary to develop standards and increase cybersecurity safeguards to protect diplomatic secrecy online.

Traditional diplomatic procedures have been significantly impacted by e-diplomacy, prompting adjustments to the new environment. The development of virtual diplomacy is one noticeable difference. Virtual conferences, webinars, and other types of online gatherings have proliferated, posing a threat to the conventional method of physical diplomacy. This transition was hastened by the COVID-19 epidemic, which forced diplomats to depend largely on virtual platforms for discussions and interactions. Due to the change in etiquette, diplomats now need to learn how to manage virtual relationships and negotiate the complexities of online diplomacy.

E-diplomacy has also changed how public diplomacy operates. Through social media, diplomats may now communicate directly with audiences throughout the world, cutting out conventional media middlemen. This offers a chance to influence public opinion, spread knowledge, and advance national narratives on a global scale. However, handling possible diplomatic crises brought on by misinformation and disinformation operations also calls for diplomats to be skilled at interpreting the complexity of online debate.

E-diplomacy is projected to have a greater future influence on conventional diplomatic procedures. Emerging developments like artificial intelligence (AI), blockchain, and virtual reality (VR) are set to influence the future of diplomacy as technology develops. Diplomats may benefit from using AI-powered technologies to help them analyze massive volumes of data, spot trends, and enhance decision-making. While VR may provide immersive virtual experiences for diplomatic conversations, blockchain technology has the ability to increase the transparency and security of diplomatic transactions.

However, as technology advances, decision-makers and diplomats must address moral and legal issues. Careful consideration will be needed when addressing issues like data privacy, AI biases, and the need for global norms and standards in the digital sphere. To guarantee the efficient and ethical use of e-diplomacy, it will be essential to strike a balance between technology improvements and diplomatic norms and procedures.

Traditional diplomatic procedures and practices have undergone a paradigm change as a result of e-diplomacy, which presents both countless benefits and important concerns. Diplomacy in the digital era has undergone a revolutionary change thanks to e-diplomacy's enhanced connectedness, effectiveness, and inclusion. To guarantee equal participation and protect diplomatic confidentially, it is crucial to overcome the digital gap and increase cybersecurity safeguards. Diplomats must learn the nuances of online interaction and adapt to virtual diplomacy. Policymakers will need to plan for and handle the ethical and regulatory ramifications of developing technology in the future. It is possible to design the future of diplomacy for the advancement of international relations by using the advantages of e-diplomacy while respecting diplomatic norms.

Chapter 7

The Digital Divide and Global Diplomacy

7. Introduction

The digital gap has become a crucial problem that connects with international diplomacy in today's linked world. The disparity in access to and use of digital technology and the internet that exists across people, communities, and countries is referred to as the "digital divide." The repercussions of this division for social advancement generally, healthcare, education, and the economy are substantial. Addressing the digital gap has emerged as a critical component of international diplomacy as the globe grows more dependent on digital technology. This article examines the complex link between the digital divide and international relations, examining the difficulties, chances, and initiatives taken by countries and international organizations to close the gap.

The digital divide is a complicated problem with many facets. One of the main factors contributing to the gap is access to digital technology like computers, cellphones, and the internet. Barriers exist in terms of infrastructure, price, and the availability of dependable internet access for many developing nations and underprivileged people. Additionally, the gap includes digital knowledge and abilities in addition to access. The digital gap is made worse by differences in gender, socioeconomic class, and education, which reduces possibilities for people and communities to fully engage in the digital era.

The digital divide has significant repercussions for international relations. Digital technologies are becoming essential instruments for communication, commerce, and diplomacy in a linked globe. Digitally advanced nations benefit significantly in terms of economic growth, innovation, and geopolitical influence. As a result, the digital gap alters the balance of power among countries, making it more difficult for them to compete fairly on the international stage. Public diplomacy is influenced by a country's ability to use digital networks and platforms to project its soft power, create narratives, and interact with audiences throughout the world. Countries without access to or control over digital technology may struggle diplomatically as a result of the digital divide.

The digital divide raises a number of difficulties that need for international diplomatic intervention. Developing the required infrastructure and ensuring that everyone has access to the internet is the first hurdle. To achieve this, it will be necessary for governments, businesses, and international organizations to work together to increase broadband network access to underserved areas. In particular in vulnerable populations, difficulties with cost and internet literacy must be addressed. Narrowing the disparity requires bridging the digital skills gap and offering training opportunities to equip people with digital literacy.

International organizations, governments, and civil society have launched a number of projects to close the digital divide after realizing its importance. By 2030, the Sustainable Development Goals (SDGs) of the United Nations must provide widespread and inexpensive internet connectivity. Global access initiatives and initiatives to promote digital literacy are coordinated by the International Telecommunication Union (ITU), a specialized UN body. Many nations have started their own national programs and plans to close the gap, concentrating on growing capacity, reforming policies, and developing infrastructure. Public-private collaborations have also been popular as powerful strategies for advancing digital inclusion since they combine the resources and know-how of both sectors.

A subset of conventional diplomacy, digital diplomacy describes the use of social media and digital platforms to interact with international audiences, influence public opinion, and further national goals. The digital divide makes it difficult for nations to successfully project their narratives and participate in public diplomacy since it restricts access to digital platforms. However, through promoting information exchange, capacity development, and international cooperation between states, digital diplomacy may also contribute to closing the gap. Countries may share best practices, encourage digital literacy, and aid in the development of partner nations' infrastructure via digital diplomacy projects.

Artificial intelligence (AI), blockchain, and the Internet of Things (IoT) are examples of emerging technologies that have the potential to change economies and society. The digital gap is exacerbated by these technologies' unequal availability. In order to solve this problem, international diplomacy must prioritize ensuring fair access to and responsible use of developing technology. To reduce the problems linked with these technologies and avoid the formation of new divisions, international collaboration and regulation are crucial. The goal of diplomatic efforts should also be to take use of new technology to close gaps and promote sustainable development.

The digital gap poses a serious problem for international diplomacy in the twenty-first century. For equitable participation in the digital era and to promote inclusive economic and social growth, it is essential to close this gap. To solve the digital gap, governments, international organizations, and the business sector must work together on diplomatic initiatives at the national and international levels. Nations may cooperate to close the digital gap and create a more inclusive and equitable digital future by encouraging universal access to digital technology, fostering digital literacy, and using digital diplomacy activities.

7.1 Investigating the digital divide and its implications for global diplomacy

With the help of rapid access to knowledge and resources, connections between individuals on other continents, and a significant transformation of the world, the digital revolution has taken place. These possibilities, however, are not available to everyone equally. The disparity between individuals who have access to digital technology and those who do not is known as the "digital divide." The impact of this gap on political engagement, economic growth, and access to healthcare, education, and healthcare has broad repercussions for international diplomacy. This article seeks to examine the digital gap, its roots and effects, and the contribution of international diplomacy to its closing.

The digital gap has many different aspects, such as accessibility to digital infrastructure, the cost of internet connection, digital literacy, and the usefulness of material. The availability of computers, broadband internet, and mobile devices is still somewhat restricted in many developing nations and underprivileged populations. This access discrepancy exacerbates already existing social, economic, and political injustices, posing a serious obstacle to advancement.

Globally, there are several variables that contribute to the digital divide. Digital technologies are difficult to acquire because of infrastructure issues including unreliable energy and spotty internet connection in rural locations. The digital gap is also significantly influenced by economic inequalities, such as poverty and income disparity. In addition, societal and cultural issues including gender disparities and a lack of educational opportunities widen the gap by restricting access to digital expertise and information.

Digital technology access is now more important than ever for competitiveness and economic success. For nations and communities without access to digital infrastructure and expertise, the digital divide provides a serious disadvantage. They are less able to use digital technologies for entrepreneurship and innovation, attract investments, and participate in the global economy. For global economic progress to be equitable and sustainable, the digital gap must be closed.

There are significant effects of the digital divide on schooling. Students' academic achievement and lifetime learning depend on their ability to access digital materials and online learning environments. However, a lot of schools in underdeveloped nations lack digital equipment and internet access. Students are deprived of important educational opportunities due to the lack of access, which also restricts their capacity to develop 21st-century skills. For people to have more power and for educational gaps to be reduced internationally, closing the digital divide in education is essential.

Access to medical services and healthcare outcomes are also impacted by the digital divide. Digital technologies, such as telemedicine, remote monitoring, and access to health information, have the potential to improve the delivery of healthcare. However, people have limited access to good healthcare, health information, and telehealth services in underprivileged locations without internet access. For bettering health outcomes and attaining universal health coverage, it is essential to reduce the digital gap in healthcare.

Politics and civic involvement may be profoundly impacted by the digital divide. People can obtain information, voice their ideas, and participate in political debate thanks to the availability of digital tools. However, underprivileged people find it difficult to receive political information, take part in democratic processes, and fight for their rights in places with poor internet connectivity. In order to ensure inclusive and participatory government globally, the digital gap must be closed.

The digital gap must be addressed in large part via international diplomacy. Sharing best practices, mobilizing resources, and creating policies to close the gap all need international engagement and cooperation. Increasing investments in digital infrastructure, supporting digital literacy initiatives, and developing collaborations between governments, businesses, and civil society groups may all be the subject of diplomatic efforts. Additionally, international diplomatic endeavors may seek to lower internet service costs and guarantee content relevance for a variety of people.

Successful projects and case studies may provide important insights into efficient methods for closing the digital gap. Examples of the beneficial effects of thorough digital policies include Rwanda's efforts in digital inclusion, Estonia's e-government initiatives, and South Korea's national broadband program. These case studies emphasize the value of political will, cross-sector cooperation, and long-term investment in the creation of digital ecosystems.

The effort of closing the digital gap is difficult and includes overcoming several obstacles. Financial limitations, a lack of infrastructure, a lack of digital awareness, and cultural obstacles are a few of the difficulties. To address these issues, officials must take a comprehensive strategy that includes infrastructure improvements, regulatory changes, training in digital skills, and specialized programs for underserved groups. In order to mobilize resources and skills to meet these difficulties, international collaboration and alliances might be very important.

The digital gap has far-reaching effects on economic growth, political engagement, education, healthcare, and other facets of international diplomacy. Governments, international organizations, civic society, and the corporate sector must work together to bridge this gap. We can build a more just and interconnected society by tackling the underlying causes of inequality and adopting inclusive and sustainable digital initiatives. To close the digital gap and guarantee a more inclusive digital future for everyone, global diplomacy must be at the forefront of encouraging cooperation, disseminating best practices, and mobilizing resources.

7.2 Examining efforts to bridge the digital divide through diplomatic initiatives

The difference between those who have access to digital technology and those who do not, known as the "digital divide," continues to be a big problem in today's linked society. Internet access, digital literacy, and the accessibility of technological infrastructure are all included in this gap. Many nations and international organizations have launched diplomatic measures to close this gap as a result of their recognition of the revolutionary potential of digital technology. With an emphasis on diplomatic endeavors, this article will analyze these activities and how well they work to close the digital gap.

It is essential to comprehend the many aspects of the digital divide before diving into diplomatic efforts to close it. The most obvious part of the digital divide is access to the internet and technical infrastructure. Many underdeveloped countries suffer with poor infrastructure and connection, whereas rich countries often claim high-speed internet access.

Additionally, bridging the digital gap depends heavily on digital literacy. Despite having access to technology, people still need to have the necessary abilities to function well online. Lack of digital literacy may prevent people from taking use of the internet's possibilities for learning, working, and making friends.

The digital gap is also significantly impacted by cost, which is another important element. The difference in access and use is made worse by the expense of devices and internet services for those living in low-income areas.

Diplomatic efforts have become an essential instrument for building global collaboration as people have come to understand the significance of closing the digital gap. In order to build a more equitable digital society, these efforts seek to address the issues of infrastructure, digital literacy, and cost.

The Sustainable Development Goals (SDGs) of the United Nations are a prominent illustration of a diplomatic endeavor. The SDGs, which were approved in 2015, include a particular goal (Goal 9.c) that states, "Significantly increase access to information and communications technology (ICT) and strive to provide universal and affordable access to the internet in least developed countries by 2020." This objective has given nations and organizations a framework for prioritizing closing the digital gap via diplomatic channels.

Additionally, international institutions like the World Bank and the International Telecommunication Union (ITU) have been instrumental in diplomatic attempts to close the digital gap. In order to improve digital access and literacy, these groups work in partnership with governments, civil society, and the corporate sector to establish strategies, policies, and funding sources.

The Global Connect Initiative is a further diplomatic effort that deserves attention. This effort, which was started in 2015, aims to connect 1.5 billion more people to the internet by 2020. In order to increase connection, affordability, and digital literacy, it highlights the value of cooperation between governments, the commercial sector, and civil society.

Cooperation, information exchange, and resource mobilization are made possible through diplomatic actions, which are crucial in closing the digital gap. Partnerships between nations may result through diplomatic initiatives, allowing for the transfer of technical know-how and resources. In order to solve the complex issues surrounding the digital divide, diplomacy may also promote communication and collaboration among stakeholders, including governments, international organizations, and the corporate sector.

Diplomacy may also affect the formulation of policies that support digital inclusion. Agreements made at the bilateral and international levels may promote spending on infrastructure improvement and the establishment of legal frameworks that support innovation and competition. Governments may also give priority to projects and programs that address the affordability of technology and internet access via diplomatic channels.

Although diplomatic efforts have the potential to close the digital gap, they are hampered by a number of issues. The complexity of the digital divide itself is a major obstacle. Addressing a number of interconnected issues, including as infrastructure, cost, and digital literacy, is necessary to close the gap. Each of these elements poses a unique set of difficulties that need for specialized strategies.

Additionally, diplomatic efforts are significantly hampered by resource limitations. Many underdeveloped nations lack the resources to invest in the programs for digital literacy and the essential infrastructure. Implementing comprehensive programs to reduce the digital gap may be expensive, and getting financing and technical help is sometimes a big challenge.

Political concerns might also hinder diplomatic attempts. International collaboration and the progress being made to close the digital gap may be hampered by geopolitical conflicts, economic disputes, and competing national interests. Additionally, countries must maintain political will and commitment, as well as congruence with domestic interests and agendas, in order to successfully carry out diplomatic endeavors.

It is difficult to evaluate how well diplomatic efforts are working to bridge the digital gap. Due to diverse socioeconomic situations and degrees of development, the effects of these projects may differ across various areas and nations. However, a number of metrics may be used to assess how successful they are.

Indicators of advancement include, but are not limited to, higher internet penetration rates and easier access to technology. The effectiveness of diplomatic endeavors may be determined by keeping an eye on the development of internet infrastructure and the number of people using it.

Second, strengthening digital skills and literacy is essential for closing the digital gap. Analyzing the accessibility and efficacy of digital literacy initiatives may help us understand how diplomatic efforts have affected this situation. Surveys and evaluations may track changes in digital literacy rates and people's aptitude for using digital technology in a variety of ways.

Thirdly, a crucial factor in the digital divide is the cost of equipment and internet connectivity. Diplomatic efforts may assist in addressing this issue by taking steps like lowering import duties on technological equipment, fostering competition in the telecoms industry, and pushing programs that provide subsidized access to technology for underserved populations. The success of such efforts may be evaluated by keeping an eye on changes in the cost of technology and internet services.

In recent years, diplomatic measures to narrow the digital gap have gained traction. Collaboration, resource mobilization, and advocacy for digital inclusion have all been aided by the United Nations, international organizations, and bilateral agreements. These efforts, despite their difficulties and limits, have the power to change societies by promoting equality in access to social participation, employment, and education. Diplomatic efforts to close the digital gap are still essential for building a more just and inclusive global digital society as the globe grows more linked.

7.3 Analyzing the impact of unequal access to technology on international relations

Technology is a critical factor in determining how international relations are shaped in a world that is becoming more linked. However, the disparity in access to technology across countries has far-reaching effects, affecting social inclusion, economic growth, and the balance of political power. In order to better understand the complex implications of uneven access to technology on international relations, this article will look at how it affects the digital gap, geopolitical power, economic inequality, and diplomacy. We can get a thorough awareness of the problems and possibilities brought forth by this digital divide by examining case studies and academic research.

The deterioration of international economic imbalances is one of the most important effects of uneven access to technology. The digital divide widens the difference between countries with developed infrastructure and those without it, preventing the latter from fully participating in the global economy. A concentration of economic power results from advanced countries gaining a competitive advantage in industries dependent on technology breakthroughs. The article will look at how uneven access to technology expands the economic gap and how it might impede the development and progress of economically underdeveloped countries.

The digital gap worsens social inequality inside countries in addition to having an influence on economic differences. Marginalized populations are unable to access possibilities for social mobility, education, and information because of unequal access to technology. In this part, we'll talk about how a lack of access to technology contributes to social exclusion, expands the wealth gap, and limits prospects for people and communities to overcome socioeconomic obstacles.

In the contemporary period, technology has emerged as a crucial factor in determining global influence. Technologically sophisticated nations often exercise influence and leverage in international affairs. The distribution of power across countries will be examined in this section in relation to uneven access to technology. It will examine case studies to show how nations with limited access to technology struggle to advance their interests in international fora and encounter vulnerabilities in a world that is becoming more and more digital. Additionally, it will look at how changes in military technology affect the balance of power and geopolitical stability.

The digital divide has changed the nature of international relations, presenting states with both difficulties and possibilities. This section will cover how uneven access to technology impacts the conduct of foreign policy and diplomatic endeavors. The emergence of digital diplomacy, the function of technology in promoting international collaboration, and the difficulties encountered by nations with weak technical infrastructure will all be covered. It will also examine how new developments in cybersecurity, information warfare, and artificial intelligence may affect diplomatic relations.

This section will examine the efforts undertaken by many stakeholders to bridge the digital gap in light of the detrimental implications that uneven access to technology has on international relations. It will look at programs and policies put in place at the national, regional, and international levels to encourage the use of technology and lessen inequalities. Case studies will provide instances of technology-driven collaboration and development that have been effective while also addressing their shortcomings.

In conclusion, there are wide-ranging and intricate effects of uneven access to technology on international relations. The digital gap exacerbates social marginalization, maintains economic inequalities, determines geopolitical power structures, and affects diplomatic relations. However, initiatives to close this gap have the potential to promote social inclusion, economic progress, and international collaboration. Policymakers and stakeholders may strive toward a more just and interconnected world where technology acts as a catalyst for improvement in international relations by assessing these potential and difficulties.

Chapter 8

Ethics and Governance in Digital Diplomacy

8. Introduction

International relations have seen a significant and revolutionary rise of digital diplomacy. Governments and diplomats all over the globe are increasingly using digital tools to conduct diplomacy and formulate foreign policy as a result of the fast growth of technology and the widespread usage of digital platforms. However, there are significant ethical and governance issues raised by this digital revolution of diplomacy. To guarantee the responsible and ethical use of digital diplomacy as it becomes a fundamental component of diplomatic relations, it is crucial to address the ethical problems and build strong governance structures.

Traditional diplomatic methods have been transformed by the emergence of digital diplomacy, which has also broadened the scope of diplomatic contacts. Diplomats may engage people, reach a larger audience, and advance their nation's interests by using social media platforms, virtual meetings, and online communication tools. Numerous possibilities exist to advance diversity, openness, and public engagement in international affairs thanks to digital diplomacy. Along with these possibilities, it also presents governance issues and moral conundrums that need for thoughtful deliberation and aggressive response.

The dissemination of misinformation and the manipulation of information are two of the main ethical issues in digital diplomacy. Digital platforms' speed and reach allow for the quick distribution of information, but they are also vulnerable to the propagation of misleading information and propaganda. The digital sphere may be used by state-sponsored actors and non-state organizations to influence political outcomes, distort public opinion, and erode confidence in diplomatic efforts. The creation of reliable procedures to validate information, advance media literacy, and counter misinformation efforts is necessary to address this ethical quandary.

The preservation of privacy and personal data is a key ethical component of digital diplomacy. Governments and embassies use digital platforms to interact with citizens, gathering and processing enormous quantities of personal data. To preserve confidence in diplomatic relations and uphold people's right to privacy, this data must be protected. To guarantee that personal data is collected, stored, and used in digital diplomacy operations in a responsible manner, governments and diplomatic organizations must create clear norms and regulations.

The ethical considerations of digital diplomacy include critical infrastructure protection and cybersecurity problems. State-sponsored actors and criminal hackers are increasingly using the digital sphere as a battlefield for their cyberattacks, focusing on diplomatic networks and communication channels. To safeguard sensitive information, uphold the integrity of diplomatic communications, and prevent unwanted access, it is essential to ensure the cybersecurity of digital diplomacy platforms and infrastructure. To prevent and combat cyber threats, governments must make significant investments in cybersecurity protections, encourage information sharing and collaboration, and create global standards and frameworks.

In addition to ethical issues, special consideration must be given to digital diplomacy governance. The conventional boundaries and jurisdictions of digital platforms are blurred, making it difficult to develop efficient governance systems. While engaged in digital diplomacy operations, diplomats must traverse a complicated world of rules, practices, and conventions. International conventions and agreements must be created in order to support ethical and responsible digital diplomacy activities while upholding country sovereignty and cultural diversity. Initiatives for increasing capacity, multilateral collaboration, and communication may enhance governance frameworks and provide a common understanding of standards for digital diplomacy.

The landscape of diplomacy has changed as a result of the quick spread of digital tools and platforms, opening up new opportunities and difficulties. For diplomatic contacts to remain credible, open, and honest, ethical aspects of digital diplomacy are essential. Governments and diplomats should take use of the advantages of digital diplomacy while reducing possible hazards by addressing ethical issues including the dissemination of misinformation, preserving privacy and personal data, and assuring cybersecurity. Furthermore, it is crucial to create governance frameworks that encourage global collaboration and debate in order to create a foundation for ethical and responsible digital diplomacy. In order to create a future in which digital diplomacy acts as a force for peace, collaboration, and mutual understanding, policymakers and diplomats must be watchful and pro-active in addressing the ethical and governance implications.

8.1 Discussing the ethical considerations and challenges in the practice of digital diplomacy

E-diplomacy, commonly referred to as cyber diplomacy, or digital diplomacy, has become an important component of contemporary international relations. In order to communicate with foreign audiences, advance their interests, and handle global crises, diplomats and governments now depend heavily on digital tools and platforms due to the fast growth of technology and the growing interconnection of the global community. However, there are a number of ethical issues and difficulties associated with the practice of digital diplomacy that should be carefully considered. This article explores issues like privacy, security, propaganda, deception, and accountability in order to talk about the ethical issues and difficulties that arise while using digital diplomacy.

Privacy is one of the most important ethical issues in digital diplomacy. Understanding target audiences, crafting messages, and influencing public opinion are all made possible by digital diplomacy, which primarily depends on data collection and analysis. Governments and embassies often gather data using a variety of techniques, such as data mining, surveillance, and social media monitoring. As people's online actions and personal information may be examined without their express agreement, privacy issues about privacy infringement are raised by the acquisition and use of personal data. This poses crucial issues about the limitations of diplomatic procedures and the defense of personal privacy rights in the digital sphere.

The use of digital diplomacy encounters major security hurdles in addition to privacy issues. Governments and embassies are more susceptible to cyber threats and assaults as they depend more on digital platforms to communicate and exchange sensitive information. The security of diplomatic communications is seriously threatened by state-sponsored hacking, espionage, and cyber warfare, which might jeopardize national security and undermine diplomatic operations. Important facets of digital diplomacy ethics include ensuring effective cybersecurity measures and encouraging international collaboration to battle cyber threats.

The employment of propaganda and false information is a crucial ethical issue in digital diplomacy. Misinformation, false news, and propaganda may sway public opinion and skew diplomatic discourse, and digital platforms have grown to be fertile ground for their spread. These channels may be used by governments and non-state entities to distribute false information, sway public opinion, or meddle in the internal affairs of other countries. This underscores the need for tactics to prevent misinformation and encourage truthful and responsible information sharing and raises questions about the legitimacy and integrity of digital diplomacy activities.

In digital diplomacy, accountability is a crucial ethical issue. It may be difficult to assign acts and hold people or organizations accountable for their online conduct due to the fluid nature of the digital world and the anonymity it provides. To guarantee openness, accountability, and ethical behavior in their digital involvement, diplomatic actors must overcome these obstacles. Crucial steps toward improving responsibility in this area include developing standards and guidelines for appropriate online conduct, encouraging international collaboration in combating digital abuses, and investigating how international law might be used to regulate digital diplomacy.

Digital diplomacy also brings up more general ethical issues with regard to the knowledge gap and access to technology. Digital platforms increase existing inequalities by giving individuals with access to technology and digital literacy a distinct advantage, even while they also provide new chances for diplomacy. To promote inclusion, equitable representation, and just participation in digital diplomatic processes, diplomatic initiatives must account for these differences. Policymakers must address the digital gap and endeavor to create a more fair and accessible digital environment in order to fully implement ethical concerns in digital diplomacy.

Digital diplomacy raises a number of ethical issues and concerns that need to be carefully considered and resolved. In the context of digital diplomacy, issues including privacy, security, propaganda, misinformation, accountability, and the digital divide present serious moral conundrums. Governments and diplomats must strike a careful balance between using digital technologies to further their diplomatic goals while upholding privacy rights, guaranteeing cybersecurity, creating accountability, and promoting factual information. The greatest interests of international diplomacy in the digital age may be served by digital diplomacy becoming a more responsible, open, and inclusive profession by addressing these ethical issues.

8.2 Examining the need for global norms and regulations to govern digital diplomacy

Diplomacy has changed significantly in the era of the internet. Traditional diplomatic procedures are changing as a result of the development of digital technology and the internet, and new modes of interaction and communication are being added. The idea of "digital diplomacy" was created as a result of this progression and refers to the use of digital tools and platforms to assist diplomatic engagements, negotiations, and public diplomacy initiatives.

Global rules and laws to guide its use are becoming more and more necessary as digital diplomacy continues to dominate and have an impact on international relations.

We will examine the causes of this need, the difficulties encountered by digital diplomacy, and the possible advantages of setting up international standards and laws in this area in this article. We intend to highlight the significance of creating a framework to direct and control digital diplomatic activities by analyzing the existing state of digital diplomacy and its consequences for global governance.

Face-to-face meetings, formal correspondence, and diplomatic missions have historically been the means of conducting diplomacy. But how diplomacy is conducted has undergone a fundamental change as a result of the digital era. The development of the internet and other digital technologies has accelerated, widened, and democratized communication. Governments and diplomats may now instantly communicate with audiences throughout the world, participate in conversations in real time, and obtain information with previously unheard-of speed and simplicity.

There are a number of reasons why digital diplomacy has become more popular. The internet has mostly developed into a potent weapon for public diplomacy, enabling governments to directly engage with foreign publics without using conventional media channels. Diplomats now use social media sites like Twitter, Facebook, and Instagram as virtual platforms to conduct public diplomacy, disseminate official remarks, and sway public opinion.

There are several advantages to using digital diplomacy in diplomatic operations. Greater accountability and openness are made possible because digital communication leaves a digital trail that can be checked and verified. Additionally, it gives governments the chance to interact with a larger variety of stakeholders, such as non-state entities and civil society groups, and reach out to new audiences. Furthermore, digital diplomacy reduces the need for substantial travel and physical presence by facilitating affordable and effective communication.

Digital diplomacy can provide certain difficulties, however. The possibility of deception, disinformation campaigns, and cyberattacks is one of the main worries. Malicious actors may easily propagate fake information, sway public opinion, and undermine diplomatic relations in the digital sphere. Furthermore, policymakers and diplomats struggle to comprehend and acclimate to new technologies and platforms, making it difficult to keep up with the rapidly changing world of digital diplomacy.

The need to protect the confidentiality and privacy of diplomatic communications is another urgent problem in digital diplomacy. Sensitive material has historically been protected by secure communication channels through traditional diplomatic channels. Assuring the integrity and secrecy of diplomatic communications, however, becomes more challenging in the digital sphere. To protect diplomatic interactions, it is vital to develop global norms and rules that set standards for secure digital communication, encryption, and data security.

Legal and jurisdictional issues are also raised by digital diplomacy. Due to the fact that the internet crosses international boundaries, it is challenging to establish legal authority and implement rules. Online diplomacy may be governed by a number of different jurisdictions, creating tensions and legal ambiguities. Clarifying the legal framework regulating digital diplomacy and fostering international collaboration to solve these issues may both be achieved by creating global standards and laws.

The balance between diplomatic restraints and freedom of speech has also come under scrutiny as a result of the advent of digital diplomacy. Digital platforms provide people the chance to express themselves and have frank conversations, but there are times when these statements may run afoul of diplomatic conventions or diplomatic sensitivities. Global norms and laws may aid in achieving a balance between the right to free speech and the diplomatic considerations required to preserve international relations.

Digital diplomacy places a high priority on ethics and accountability. The speed and anonymity of internet communication may sometimes encourage the spread of offensive language, harassment, or hate speech. Global norms and rules, which place an emphasis on ideas like respect for human rights, inclusion, and the advancement of peace and stability, may provide diplomats guidelines for conducting ethical and responsible digital diplomacy.

Digital diplomacy plays a significant role in contemporary diplomacy and presents both possibilities and difficulties.

Global standards and laws must be established in order to maximize the benefits of digital diplomacy while minimizing its perils. Such standards and guidelines may safeguard the confidentiality and security of diplomatic communications, handle issues of law and jurisdiction, strike a balance between the right to free speech and diplomatic restraints, and advance moral and responsible digital diplomacy. The international community may profit from this emerging practice while preserving the integrity of diplomatic ties in the digital era by creating a thorough framework to regulate it.

8.3 Addressing issues related to privacy, data protection, and surveillance in digital diplomacy

In today's linked world, dealing with privacy, data protection, and surveillance problems in digital diplomacy has become a crucial concern. Governments and international organizations are increasingly using digital platforms to conduct diplomatic operations and interact with one another as technology progresses. But this digital transition also carries with it a number of issues with regard to monitoring, data security, and privacy. The significance of addressing these concerns in the context of digital diplomacy, the dangers and repercussions of insufficient privacy protections, and the tactics and techniques that may be used to defend privacy and data protection in digital diplomacy are all covered in this article.

Digital diplomacy is the practice of conducting diplomatic operations and improving communication between countries and international organizations while using digital technologies such as social media, websites, and online forums. These technological advancements have completely changed how diplomacy is carried out since they enable in-the-moment communication, quick information sharing, and elevated public participation. However, they also provide security holes that may be used by bad actors to access private data without authorization or carry out surveillance operations. To guarantee the accuracy and security of diplomatic communications, it is vital that privacy and data protection problems in digital diplomacy be addressed.

The safeguarding of sensitive data and information shared between diplomatic institutions is one of the main issues in digital diplomacy. Negotiations, private conversations, and the exchange of sensitive information are frequent components of diplomatic contacts. Any invasion of privacy or unlawful access to this information might have serious repercussions, harming both domestic and foreign security. Additionally, the privacy of diplomats and their capacity to have open and honest talks may be seriously threatened by the monitoring capabilities of certain nations and non-state entities. As a result, strong safeguards must be in place to ensure the privacy and secrecy of diplomatic communications in the digital sphere.

The security of people's personal information is a crucial component in dealing with privacy, data protection, and surveillance concerns in digital diplomacy. Diplomats often divulge personal information, such as names, contact details, and affiliations, while using internet platforms. If this information is managed improperly or is obtained by unauthorized parties, it may result in identity theft and privacy violations. Furthermore, privacy issues and the possibility of manipulation or discrimination might arise from the acquisition and aggregation of personal data by digital platforms for targeted advertising or monitoring reasons. In order to guarantee that personal information is handled safely and morally in the context of digital diplomacy, extensive data protection laws and policies are required.

Inadequate privacy protections in digital diplomacy may have far-reaching effects. Diplomatic crises may result from a single data leak or privacy violation that erodes trust in digital platforms and between diplomatic bodies. Furthermore, the disclosure of sensitive material may have long-lasting political, economic, or societal repercussions. In the past, for instance, the unauthorised leaking of diplomatic cables resulted in serious diplomatic ramifications and strained ties between nations. Therefore, it is crucial to address privacy and data protection concerns early on in order to reduce the risks and possible repercussions linked to insufficient protections.

In the context of digital diplomacy, a number of tactics and approaches may be used to solve these issues. To safeguard the secrecy and integrity of diplomatic communications, it is crucial to use strong encryption and secure communication protocols. Secure key management procedures and powerful encryption algorithms may considerably improve the security of digital platforms and stop illegal access to critical data.

To address privacy and data protection in digital diplomacy, regulatory frameworks and international agreements are just as important as technical solutions. The collecting, storage, and use of personal data in diplomatic operations should be governed by explicit norms and standards that are jointly established by governments and international organizations. A consistent framework for resolving privacy issues and guaranteeing uniformity in data protection policies across nations may be found in international accords like data protection treaties.

Additionally, it is crucial to educate ambassadors and diplomatic staff members on privacy and data protection best practices and to provide them with the necessary training. To provide ambassadors the information and skills they need to safely traverse the digital world, diplomatic training programs should include courses on digital security, privacy awareness, and responsible use of digital platforms.

In order to overcome privacy and data protection issues in digital diplomacy, public-private collaborations may be very helpful. Governments, international organizations, and technology businesses working together can make it easier to create safe digital platforms, share best practices, and set up accountability systems. These parties may jointly handle the intricate and dynamic nature of privacy and data protection problems in digital diplomacy by cooperating.

In today's linked world, it is crucial to address concerns about privacy, data protection, and monitoring in digital diplomacy. Protecting privacy and data protection is essential to ensuring the security, integrity, and efficacy of diplomatic communications as technology continues to influence how diplomacy is conducted. Governments and international organizations can successfully address these issues and pave the way for a secure and privacy-respecting digital diplomacy environment by putting in place strong encryption measures, creating legal frameworks, raising awareness, and encouraging collaboration among stakeholders.

Chapter 9

The Future of Digital Diplomacy

9. Introduction

Diplomacy has long been a pillar for preserving friendly ties and settling disputes between countries in the dynamic world of international relations. Diplomats have traditionally conducted formal gatherings, face-to-face conversations, and negotiating procedures. But as the globe has become more linked and technology has advanced quickly, a new kind of diplomacy has emerged: digital diplomacy. The use of digital tools and technology to enable diplomatic contact, information sharing, and relationship development between nations is referred to as digital diplomacy, sometimes known as e-diplomacy or cyber diplomacy.

Digital diplomacy has grown significantly over the last several decades and revolutionized international relations between governments. The growth of the internet, social media sites, and other digital technologies has given diplomats new ways to interact with audiences abroad, advance national interests, and influence public opinion. Digital diplomacy has a bright future and will continue to influence how international relations develop in the years to come.

The future of digital diplomacy is being influenced by a number of factors, including the growing significance of information and communication technologies (ICTs) in world affairs. ICTs have significantly changed not just how individuals interact, but also how everyone has access to information. Because of this accessibility, people may now participate in diplomatic procedures and voice their thoughts on important global concerns. States must thus adjust to this shifting environment and make efficient use of digital resources to communicate with a larger audience and present their national narratives.

The conventional diplomatic toolkit will probably use digital diplomacy more in the future. Digital diplomacy will be seen as an integral part of diplomatic efforts rather than as a distinct entity. To effectively manage digital diplomacy activities, diplomatic missions will need to spend in developing a solid digital infrastructure, educating diplomats in digital skills, and setting up specialized departments or divisions. Through this connection, ambassadors will be able to switch between physical and digital platforms with ease, taking use of both platforms' advantages to further their diplomatic goals.

Furthermore, big data analytics and artificial intelligence (AI) will become more prevalent in diplomatic operations in the future of digital diplomacy. Artificial intelligence (AI)-enabled systems may assist diplomats in collecting and analyzing massive quantities of data, spotting trends, and learning about global trends and public attitude. Diplomats will be able to anticipate possible disputes and crises thanks to this data-driven strategy, which will also help them make better judgments and target their tactics to certain audiences. Additionally, AI has the potential to automate mundane diplomatic activities like translation, analysis, and surveillance, freeing up diplomats' time to concentrate on more strategic negotiation and higher-level strategic thinking.

Future iterations of digital diplomacy will depend heavily on social media platforms. These websites have become into potent instruments for state actors to interact with audiences abroad, distribute information, and create narratives. In order to successfully explain their ideas, combat misinformation campaigns, and interact with significant online groups, governments will need to create sophisticated social media strategies. It will also be crucial for nations and social media businesses to work together to solve problems like privacy, security, and the dissemination of false information.

Furthermore, virtual diplomacy and immersive technology will become more common in the future of digital diplomacy. Through the creation of immersive and interactive experiences, virtual reality (VR) and augmented reality (AR) have the potential to redefine diplomatic interaction. Meetings, conferences, and discussions that take place virtually may become the norm, decreasing the need for physical travel and enhancing diplomats' ability to communicate with colleagues throughout the globe. Additionally, VR and AR may help with people-to-people diplomacy, tourist marketing, and cultural exchanges, promoting understanding and bridging gaps between countries.

However, there are important dangers and concerns associated with the future of digital diplomacy that must be taken into consideration. The digital gap among communities and across nations is one of the main issues. Digital technologies are not available to all countries equally, and differences in connection might pose obstacles to the efficient use of digital diplomacy. International collaboration, infrastructure spending, and policies that support digital inclusion will be necessary to close this gap.

The privacy and security of digital communication routes is another issue. The danger of cyberattacks, data breaches, and information manipulation rises as digital diplomacy becomes more common. States will need to make significant investments in cybersecurity protections, create secure communication methods, and enhance international norms and rules regulating cyberspace.

The use of digital diplomacy in the future has the power to drastically alter how nations interact with one another and the general public. Diplomatic practices and tactics will change as a result of the integration of digital tools, AI, big data analytics, and immersive technology. To guarantee that digital diplomacy is inclusive and successful, it is essential to handle the risks and problems that come with it. States can negotiate the challenges of the digital era and establish more solid diplomatic links in the future by using technology and embracing digital innovation.

9.1 Speculating on the future trajectory of digital diplomacy

Digital diplomacy has become a vital instrument for countries to participate in international relations and formulate their foreign policy in today's networked world. The way diplomats interact, communicate, and negotiate with one another and their counterparts has changed dramatically as a result of the quick development of technology and the extensive acceptance of digital platforms. It is essential to make predictions about the future trajectory of digital diplomacy and investigate any possible effects it could have on international relations as we negotiate the always changing terrain of world politics. This article seeks to explore the opportunities and difficulties that may arise as we enter the digital age of diplomacy.

International relations have traditionally been based on diplomacy, which makes it easier for governments to communicate and negotiate. The emergence of the digital era, however, has altered the diplomatic scene by opening up new channels and resources for communication. The development of digital diplomacy has been quick and varied, starting with the early usage of email and electronic communication and continuing with the rise of social media and virtual diplomacy. This paragraph will examine the significant turning points in the history of digital diplomacy, emphasizing how it has changed the way that diplomacy is conducted and created new opportunities for statecraft.

The capacity to promote worldwide communication is one of digital diplomacy's most important accomplishments. Social media platforms like Twitter and Facebook have given diplomats an unprecedented level of audience reach and real-time communication. In this section, we'll talk about how digital platforms have transformed public diplomacy by enabling diplomats to interact directly with the public, exchange knowledge, and sway opinion. The difficulties of using social media in diplomacy will also be covered, including the necessity for cautious message and the danger of false information.

The COVID-19 epidemic has expedited the growth of virtual diplomacy by forcing diplomats to get used to distant labor and online conversations. Maintaining diplomatic interactions amid crises has grown dependent on virtual platforms like video conferencing software. The effect of virtual diplomacy on future diplomatic discussions will be discussed in this paragraph, including any possible gains in effectiveness, accessibility, and inclusion. The difficulties of conducting discussions virtually, such as establishing trust, upholding secrecy, and guaranteeing clear communication, will also be covered.

Diplomats are faced with previously unheard-of possibilities and problems as a result of the exponential expansion of data and the development of artificial intelligence. This section will go through how big data analytics and AI may be used to improve diplomatic operations, from spotting possible conflicts to anticipating geopolitical trends. It will examine the moral issues surrounding data security and privacy in digital diplomacy as well as the need for global standards and laws to control the use of these technologies. It will also look at how AI-powered chatbots may be used in public diplomacy and diplomatic exchanges.

A key component of diplomacy for a long time has been soft power, or the capacity to influence people by appeal and persuasion rather than violence. This paragraph will examine how digital diplomacy might improve a country's projection of soft power. It will explore how a country's culture, values, and policies may be promoted via the use of digital media, influencing views abroad and fostering diplomatic ties. The paragraph will also go through the difficulties in maintaining a country's internet image and fending against misinformation online.

It is certain that digital diplomacy will continue to play a crucial role in reshaping the diplomatic environment as we look to the future of international relations. Digital platforms, virtual diplomacy, big data analytics, and artificial intelligence have the potential to provide diplomats with strong tools to improve soft power projection, negotiation, and communication. The need for international standards and laws, cybersecurity dangers, and ethical issues are just a few of the many difficulties that this transformation also brings with it. Nations must adjust to this shifting environment, invest in digital infrastructure, and promote collaboration to handle the new possibilities and problems if they are to fully achieve the promise of digital diplomacy. We may proactively traverse this digital era and create a more effective and inclusive global diplomatic framework by speculating on the future course of digital diplomacy.

9.2 Identifying emerging trends and technologies that will shape the future of diplomatic practice

A pillar of international relations for millennia has been diplomacy, the art of conducting discussions between states. The profession of diplomacy must change to handle new problems and capture new possibilities as the globe quickly changes and becomes more interconnected. Finding and comprehending new trends and technologies that have the potential to alter how diplomacy is practiced in the future is a crucial component of this adaptability. This article tries to examine the key developments in fashion, science, and technology that will probably have an influence on diplomacy in the next years.

In order to reflect the shifting dynamics of the international scene, diplomacy has been continually developing. In the past, negotiations and state-to-state engagements were the main priorities of diplomacy. However, in recent years, a wider variety of players, including non-state groups, civil society organizations, and multinational businesses, have become part of diplomacy. This expanding breadth calls for a proactive strategy to recognize and comprehend new trends and technologies that may have an impact on diplomatic practice.

Unprecedented levels of interconnectedness have been made possible by the onset of globalization and the quick development of technology. These changes have made it easier for information, ideas, and people to freely move across borders, which presents diplomatic possibilities and difficulties. The emergence of digital diplomacy and the effect of social media on public diplomacy initiatives are two examples of how developing trends and technologies that allow increased connectedness and their possible consequences for diplomacy must be kept in mind by diplomats.

Machine learning and artificial intelligence (AI) are set to alter a number of facets of diplomacy. Huge volumes of data may be analyzed by AI-powered algorithms, allowing diplomats to gain insights and make better judgments. These technologies can also help with trend forecasting, pattern detection, and risk assessment, which will improve diplomatic forecasting and strategic planning. To guarantee accountability and responsible usage, however, it is important to thoroughly analyze the ethical issues and possible hazards related to the use of AI in diplomacy.

Nations are now facing new dangers and difficulties as a result of their increasing dependence on digital technology, notably in the area of cybersecurity. Diplomats must be knowledgeable about cybersecurity challenges and endeavor to create global standards and methods for the protection of sensitive data and vital infrastructure. Additionally, as more diplomats use social media platforms, online forums, and virtual meetings to further their goals, the advent of digital diplomacy has created new opportunities for participation and impact.

The area of big data analytics has emerged as a result of the accessibility of enormous volumes of data, providing diplomats with hitherto unheard-of capabilities for decision-making based on facts. Diplomats may recognize patterns, spot new trends, and foresee impending crises by using predictive analytics. Effective data management and interpretation may greatly improve diplomatic efforts, from trade and economic discussions to the prevention and settlement of conflicts.

Diplomacy is essential in combating climate change, which has emerged as one of the most important global concerns of our time. As governments cooperate to lessen the consequences of climate change, negotiate international accords, and promote sustainable development, there will unavoidably be a growing emphasis on environmental diplomacy in future diplomatic practice. To successfully contribute to this crucial field, diplomats must get acquainted with the newest trends and technology in renewable energy, green infrastructure, and climate resilience.

Numerous new trends and technology will influence diplomatic practice in the future, necessitating a proactive and flexible attitude. Diplomats must be diligent in seeing and comprehending these changes, which range from the increased interconnection brought on by globalization to the revolutionary possibilities of AI, cybersecurity, big data analytics, and environmental diplomacy. Diplomats may take use of their potential to improve diplomatic efforts, promote international collaboration, and meet the difficult problems of the twenty-first century by embracing these new trends and technology.

9.3 Considering the potential impact of artificial intelligence, virtual reality, and blockchain on digital diplomacy

The areas of artificial intelligence (AI), virtual reality (VR), and blockchain have emerged as disruptive forces with tremendous potential to transform numerous facets of society in today's linked and fast expanding digital ecosystem. Digital diplomacy stands out among these disciplines as one that may gain a lot from the use of these technologies. The use of digital tools, platforms, and technology to advance diplomatic endeavors, advance international relations, and increase international cooperation is referred to as "digital diplomacy."

Diplomats and other international players are increasingly using digital platforms and communication channels as a means of navigating the complexity of the global scene. In the digital era, AI, VR, and blockchain provide special potential to handle diplomatic issues, improve communication, and foster transparency and trust. This essay seeks to provide a thorough examination of the possible advantages and difficulties connected with the use of these technologies to the field of digital diplomacy.

Digital diplomacy, commonly referred to as e-diplomacy or cyber diplomacy, is the practice of conducting diplomatic operations via the use of online platforms and digital technology. It includes a broad variety of operations, such as managing digital diplomacy networks, public diplomacy, and diplomatic communication. The fast development of technology has had a considerable influence on diplomatic procedures, making the use of digital tools necessary to successfully meet current diplomatic difficulties.

Digital diplomacy might be transformed by artificial intelligence thanks to its superior analytical skills, automated decision-making, and intelligent data processing. AI can help diplomats analyze massive volumes of data to acquire insights, see trends, and forecast them. This may help in the creation of policies, crisis management, and decision-making processes. Additionally, chatbots and virtual assistants powered by AI may improve diplomatic communication by offering in-context translation, individualized support, and effective information retrieval.

By building virtual settings that mimic real-world circumstances, virtual reality may change diplomatic communication thanks to its immersive and interactive features. Meetings, conferences, and negotiations may take place virtually, bridging geographic distances and promoting diversity. Additionally, virtual reality (VR) may promote cross-cultural interactions by letting ambassadors gain empathy by directly experiencing other cultures. VR may also be used to public diplomacy projects, giving diplomats new and effective methods to interact with audiences throughout the world.

Blockchain technology, which is renowned for being open and decentralized, has the potential to significantly improve trust and transparency in digital diplomacy. Blockchain-based solutions can guarantee the accuracy of official documents, protect sensitive data, and stop manipulation or modification. Blockchain-enabled smart contracts may simplify diplomatic agreements and discussions by automating procedures and cutting down on bureaucracy. Blockchain can also facilitate digital identity verification, reducing the risk of fraud or impersonation.

While the combination of blockchain, VR, and AI has tremendous promise for digital diplomacy, there are also a number of possibilities and difficulties to be taken into account. Opportunities include more openness, data-driven decision-making, better efficiency, and improved communication. To enable the responsible and fair deployment of new technologies, however, issues including ethical ramifications, data privacy issues, technical infrastructure needs, and the digital gap must be properly addressed.

Blockchain, virtual reality, and artificial intelligence have a significant and disruptive potential influence on digital diplomacy. These technological advancements provide exceptional chances to improve intergovernmental relations, boost cultural understanding, increase openness, and strengthen international trust. The related difficulties and moral issues must, however, be carefully taken into account when integrating these technologies. Digital diplomacy may develop to suit the needs of the digital age and contribute to a more interconnected and cooperative global society by appropriately using these technologies.

Chapter 10

Conclusion: Redefining Diplomatic Frontiers

The dynamics of diplomacy are continually changing in the modern, fast-paced, and networked world. A variety of global trends, from technology improvements to evolving geopolitical landscapes, are challenging traditional views of diplomatic borders, tactics, and aims. It is important to consider the main findings and developing trends that have impacted our knowledge of contemporary diplomacy as we come to the conclusion of our thorough investigation of the subject of redefining diplomatic borders. The important points made during the discussion are summarized in this conclusion, which also offers a look forward at how diplomatic borders could change in the years to come.

The traditional definition of diplomacy, which restricted it to interactions between nations via official representatives, has undergone major change recently. The range of diplomatic involvement has increased with the advent of non-state entities including multinational businesses, civil society groups, and international institutions. In addition to revolutionizing diplomatic relations' speed and scope, the development of digital communication technology has also put conventional hierarchies and power structures to the test. These modifications underline the need of redefining diplomatic borders in order to include new players and adjust to the continuously changing global environment.

The significance of multilateral diplomacy as a strategy for addressing complicated global concerns has increased as a result of the increasing interconnectivity of states. For diplomatic talks and consensus-building, multilateral institutions like the United Nations and regional organizations have become essential venues. Redefining diplomatic borders in this environment entails enhancing and modernizing these institutions to guarantee their efficacy and inclusiveness. Additionally, it calls for the creation of fresh global institutions to deal with recent problems like climate change, cybersecurity, and public health.

Economic diplomacy has emerged as a key component of contemporary foreign policy as economic interconnectedness continues to increase. National interests are being pursued via economic cooperation, trade talks, and investment plans rather than only through military or political means. Utilizing economic tools to accomplish diplomatic goals, encouraging partnerships and regional integration, and tackling economic inequality on a global scale are all part of redefining diplomatic boundaries in the area of economics.

The revolution in communication, data interchange, and information management brought about by technological improvements has had a significant influence on diplomacy. Through the use of digital platforms and social media, real-time interaction and public involvement have completely changed how diplomacy is done. These changes do, however, also bring with them problems, such cybersecurity risks and the possibility for misinformation campaigns. Using technology for diplomatic goals while upholding moral and responsible use requires redefining diplomatic limits in the digital era.

It is impossible to exaggerate the value of soft power and cultural diplomacy in today's linked globe. In an effort to shape worldwide views, nations are actively using cultural exchanges, public diplomacy, and the projection of national narratives and ideals. In this context, redefining diplomatic borders entails appreciating the value of soft power and funding cultural diplomacy projects that foster international collaboration, respect, and understanding.

Global security concerns, such as terrorism, the spread of WMD, cyberthreats, and pandemics, need for an all-encompassing and cooperative strategy. Strengthening diplomatic efforts to avert wars, enable disarmament, and advance stability are necessary for redefining diplomatic borders in the area of security. To successfully confront new security threats, it also calls for increased coordination across governmental, military, intelligence, and law enforcement organizations.

In conclusion, the idea of diplomatic boundaries is significantly changing in response to how the contemporary world is changing. Diplomatic interactions are being reshaped by a number of important variables, including the evolving character of diplomacy, the expansion of multilateralism, economic interdependence, technical breakthroughs, soft power, and threats to international security. A comprehensive strategy that values inclusion, creativity, and collaboration among many players is necessary to redefine diplomatic borders. As time goes on, it will be necessary for diplomats, decision-makers, and people throughout the world to adjust to these new realities and jointly manage the intricacies of a diplomatic environment that is fast changing. By doing this, we may successfully solve the important issues of our day and create a society that is more tranquil, affluent, and integrated.

Refrences

Beasley, R. (2018). Digital diplomacy: Understanding foreign policy in the digital age. Routledge.

1. Gilboa, E. (2018). Digital diplomacy: Theory and practice. Routledge.

2. Seib, P. (2018). Digital diplomacy: Conversations on innovation in foreign policy. Routledge.

3. Snow, N., & Taylor, P. M. (Eds.). (2016). Routledge handbook of public diplomacy. Routledge.

4. Wiseman, G. (2019). Is digital diplomacy making us dumber? In Search of a Digital Diplomatic Dividend (pp. 7-26). Springer.

5. Khamis, S., Ang, L., & Welling, R. (Eds.). (2017). Digital diplomacy: Theory and practice (Vol. 7). Routledge.

6. Manor, I. (2016). The digital diplomacy handbook: How to use social media to engage with global audiences. Rowman & Littlefield.

7. Melissen, J. (Ed.). (2017). The new public diplomacy: Soft power in international relations. Springer.

8. High-Level Panel on Digital Cooperation. (2019). The age of digital interdependence. United Nations.

9. Corneliu, B. (2017). Cybersecurity in international relations: An introduction. Polirom.

10. Sharp, P. (2017). Digital diplomacy and international relations: A primer for the 21st century. Routledge.

11. Zaharna, R. S. (2019). Digital diplomacy: Theory and practice (2nd ed.). Routledge.

12. Gilboa, E. (2017). Public diplomacy in a digital age. Oxford Research Encyclopedia of Communication.

13. Djerejian, E. (2018). Digital diplomacy in an era of global information flows. In Global Diplomacy in the 21st Century (pp. 61-81). Springer.

14. Bjola, C., & Holmes, M. (2015). Digital diplomacy: Theory and practice. Contemporary Security Policy, 36(2), 1-21.

15. Jönsson, C., & Hallin, D. C. (Eds.). (2018). Communication, media and the public sphere. Walter de Gruyter GmbH & Co KG.

16. Seib, P. (2012). Real-time diplomacy: Politics and power in the social media era. Macmillan.

17. Pascal, A. (2016). Digital diplomacy as a tool of public diplomacy: Assessing social media impact

on diplomatic practice. *Diplomacy & Statecraft,* 27(2), 292-308.

18. Manheim, J. B., & Rich, R. C. (2017). The challenge of digital diplomacy. *The Hague Journal of Diplomacy,* 12(1-2), 1-11.

19. Zaharna, R. S., Arsenault, A. M., & Fisher, A. (Eds.). (2014). *Relational, networked and collaborative approaches to public diplomacy: The Connective Mindshift.* Routledge.